In this Volume....

Editor's Note: Well Volume 4 of the Spinner Magazine Worldwide is here and I hope you all will enjoy it

I put a lot of work into this issue to get it out I think it has turned out good. Let me know what you think.
I had a type in the last issue as part of Eric Laidler's interview where I used a bird pic that was one of Hannes Rossouw's foundation birds by accident and said the bird was one of Eric's.

Please let me know what you think of this issue as I would enjoy hearing from you all.

To contact me please send your emails to; davesrollerpigeons@gmail.com

Until Next Time...
Dave

Feeding Fundamentals
By
Dave Henderson

Many years ago when I first started flying competition here in Northern California many of the fanciers around here were preaching to use a 50/50 mix of wheat and milo to fly their kit birds on. I fed this mix religiously and eventually realized that while feeding this mix it appeared that over time the birds would eventually reach a plateau where it didn't seem to matter how much of this mix you gave the birds they always seemed to be starving and many times the kits being fed like this would prone to DQ on fly day. I also noticed the feather quality on the birds could be very bad and seemed to be deteriorating as well giving you fragile feathers that could break off during rolling.

Several years after this a local roller flyer who was also a nutritionist, Paul Mabie, took the time to analyze this 50/50 mix of wheat and milo. He wrote a small book about feeding rollers and several articles in the Northern California Roller Club bulletins about feeding practices with our rollers. I had never really paid attention to what was best to feed our birds at the time as a wheat and milo mix was very cheap in those days and this was the mix that many were preaching about feeding with. I just assumed this veteran fanciers new best at this time of what to feed.

After Paul exposed me to the proper way to keep the birds healthy with the various feeds I began to see great strides in my own birds in reliability and optimal performance. I think it is not bad to feed adult birds this mix of wheat and milo but with young birds just developing muscle and learning how to roll this is a different story. Young birds need to be fed a well-balanced diet so that they can develop properly and become strong adult birds or hold over birds with some. This seems like it has been many years since I was first exposed to Paul's ideals but I can assure you this is the right path for our rollers. Nutrition is everything with athletics and our rollers are indeed athletes.

Feeding our performing rollers always seems to be a process that we end up refining all the time as we are breeding and flying our rollers. We end up experimenting and learning more as we go which is expected in this hobby that is continually in motion in terms of learning and it has always been like this. Even looking back over all the articles that Bill Pensom wrote about these amazing birds over his term, you could see he was also learning throughout his "career" with the rollers. So it's just unrealistic to think that at some point we will KNOW IT ALL. Sharing ideals and methods is what makes this hobby what it is today for those that choose to pay attention.

There are so many variables that can affect feeding and this will include climate and geography obviously. So what works for me here in Redding, California may not work where you live. Much to feeding is even affected by what family of birds you are working with, the individual metabolism in specific families can also vary. I think experimenting with various feeding practices until we are able to find a system that will work day in and day out with our performing rollers is totally normal. I think it's important to find a system that is easily incorporated as you are more apt to keep using a system that is easy and not complicated. I have read some articles of guys prepping their kit birds for 2-3 weeks, or more, to get that peak performance. Knowing the fundamentals can get someone to learning how and what to give their own birds to move forward.

I was very surprised to find that there are some areas of the US that don't have all the available grains as I have here and many areas don't even offer mixed grains specifically for our pigeons. This kind of seems foreign to me as it's always been that way here in Northern California, when I started raising pigeons they even came in 100 lb. bags back then. In the areas that do not have all the grains you will have to improvise a feeding program that uses what you have available in your area and it will be likely that you will need to give regular supplements to keep the birds healthy because of this. I know some that feed chicken pellets to their pigeons with no real issues, but chickens are larger than pigeons and can get overdosed with specific vitamins and minerals which can affect them negatively as well.

Here in Northern California we literally have all the needed grains at our disposal (California is a huge agricultural area) and my main mix is labeled 15.5% with no corn made by Winner's Cup. This is the not the best feed in the world but it's consistently good for the price and there is really no other option unless I buy individual grains separately and mix my own, which is not a bad option if you ask me. The only downside to individual grains is storage and cost. I have tried better quality feeds but these are no longer available in my immediate area and the same feed can vary from $6-8 difference per bag from one feed store to the next. I would actually try any mix that has NO corn as I find corn is not needed here, doesn't get cold enough. Corn will cause, at least in my birds, rollers to fly excessively high and I don't like that so I have discontinued feeding any corn. This is either popcorn or the whole corn (large variety). I might use a little corn during the coldest months here but its short term and while the birds are on lock down.

This 15% with no corn mix I use contains; Wheat, Red & White Milo, Maple Peas, Austrian Peas, Trapper Peas, Safflower Seed, Oat Groats, Paddy Rice and Vetch. The largest percentage of seed seems to be wheat to me by looking at it and there is a fair amount of safflower also. My birds pretty much eat everything in the mix except for the wheat which is a poor quality wheat on average, some sort of white wheat. It's not the nice red wheat that you can get separately in 50lb bags, it appears to me the mixed feed has some lower quality grains in them certain times of year. I even see some blackish wrinkled up peas at times and the birds don't eat them either but they don't put these in much.

I also purchase separate bags of milo and even Austrian Peas at times to supplement my feed mainly for the kit birds. I also recently started using an 18% extruded round pigeon pellet this season to also assist with the health of kit birds as a substitute of peas mostly due to the price of peas lately. So far this product seems to be doing the trick but you have to keep a watchful eye on all the newer babies as they leave the nest until they learn healthy eating habits. This means feeding some individual grains to your birds separately to insure they are getting a healthy diet. I am also giving Austrian Peas or these Extruded pigeon pellets first to my kit birds at least 2 days a week I have no problems with birds going light etc... I also give them grit about once per month in small quantities.

I have asked how others feed their kit birds in other countries such as the UK or Ireland and they have always fed their birds with individual grains, usually giving them barley first. Barley is not commonly used here in the US but I think many are now using it. It is also said to keep the birds down to a good height. I never did ask if the fanciers in the UK/Ireland feed barley a lot because of cost or just because this is what they have learned over the years and was passed down from elder pigeon breeders before them? I will ask this to some and see what is said.

I have recently discovered that even though my birds are getting the proper amount of amino acids from the mix I use this is still not a balanced diet, especially for breeding birds. It seems that the various grains contain many of the needed vitamins and minerals our birds need, but iodine is not part of this and is a much needed product to our birds and especially in the stock loft. Humans as you know also need iodine in their diets. **See my article in this issue talking more details of iodine in our pigeons' diets in the "Medicine Chest" section.**

I keep telling myself that I want to switch my breeders over to pellets and find it difficult to do this, some birds eat the pellets fine, but others despise them so keeping with grain seems to be the most logical thing under those conditions. I think if I continue to supplement kit birds with them that over time the birds will all get used to them this way and this will eventually give me the ability to give my breeders pellets also, but it will not happen overnight.

There is also a cost issue and more cleaning when using pellets. The cost I think is offsetting as you don't need the other supplements or grit but the mess is something else altogether. These pellets are obviously healthier for our birds and an all in one product, the babies are healthier because of them leaving the nest. Pellets have everything our birds need to include grit, vitamins and all needed minerals. By feeding grain to your stock birds we know we are going to need to give supplements in their water or feed throughout the year to keep our birds healthy and stress free. So I see the benefits of pellets but have still not transitioned to pellets yet.

Many of the modern flyers/breeders, especially here in the US, have now begun to keep a better watch of how the birds are in terms of health, especially with kit birds. Proper feeding can survive you more birds and create less culls in the long run, which will also lead you to breeding less birds overall. Breeding too many birds is probably worse than breeding not enough as you get a point at which you cannot really manage the birds properly when you have too many.

I have seen many ways that guys can insure the birds get their fair share of feed to include feeding them one on one or even in a type of "stall system" where you can plug in each members in your 20 bird team into a specific small cage or stall so they get the feed they need. Many hard working birds demand more feed but are unable to get this due to others that might eat quicker than they do so this why some do this to insure our best spinners have everything they need to perform well. So at times it is best to pull out the top performers and feed them individually until they get their fill, this will keep up their strength and keep them going strong.

Much of the issues with our breeders here in the United States is that by tossing in a mixed grain of various seeds, some birds begin to "cherry pick" specific grains they like more than others, namely the milo at my loft. So I am forced to feed separate grains several times a week to insure my kit birds stay healthy. I have had on several occasions over the last 2 seasons where I have had birds roll down and when I go to retrieve them I discover they are extremely light in weight and are obviously not in healthy state. Should the bird survive the impact I have been able to place these birds in small individual pens so I can feed them up and monitor their health more closely. This is when I noticed these birds are eating more milo than any other seed on average. So it's the lack of a proper diet in terms of amino acids that is affecting these specific birds the most. If you do feed grains the birds they must eat at least 3 grains to get enough of the right amino acids to sustain good health and if I did use just 3 grains these grains would be wheat, milo and Austrian Peas. If you are unable to insure your birds are eating these 3 grains in enough quantities to remain healthy then you will have to give some sort of vitamin supplements to insure they stay healthy or like many of our overseas flyers do, give them to the birds individually starting with the grains they dislike the most.

I have been using some larger feeder cup that are harder for the birds to kick or sweep the feed out of it. This is a small feeder made by Crown, see photo below. This feeder can hold a lot of feed and I give 1 to each of my pairs in their own boxes. I put in an amount everyday for the birds and after about 3 days I will dump this container into another air tight container to save for my kit birds. I find the breeders don't like the wheat at all and at times will leave Maple peas and a little milo too. So when I dump this mix into a separate container I will use this "extra feed" for the kit birds at a future date and this also works as off season feed as well for the birds in separation. I will simply just mix in some of my normal 15% mix to this and maybe a little more milo and call his my kit bird mix which should be somewhere around a 14-15% mix. As I mentioned I give the Extruded pellets separately a couple times a week before I give the mix.

This is the individual feeders I have in each breeding box for my pairs

I think for the kit birds it's really not so much what you feed as how much you feed and many just simply overfeed the birds. Overfeeding will do more to prevent and slow down the development not to mention cause them to pick up bad habits as well. These would include staying out after they land from a flight and not rushing in or even pairing up on the roof and not wanting to go in due to being over fed. Our rollers are habitual and if you feed them the right amount every day they will be healthy and manageable, but if you don't they can cause you a lot of headaches.

Overfeeding will firstly encourage pairing up and laying eggs in your kit boxes. This is really not safe for our hens as they can possibly blowing out their sex organs should they be egg bound when you fly them and hit a high velocity spin at the same time. The egg is a separate part of the body and will literally blow out their rectum which will probably cause them to be at the very least sterile for the rest of their lives and they could even die from infection with such an injury.

I think the starting point for kit birds is approximately 1 tablespoon per bird. This is not set in stone and some birds will demand more and so long as they are performing well and remain manageable then you probably have the proper amount of feed going to them. I cannot really tell you what this amount will be and you will need to experiment a bit. A good rule of thumb is if the birds are flying and rolling well for at least 45 minutes then you probably have a good thing going. If the birds are flying excessive and or not remaining manageable like mentioned above you are no doubt overfeeding. You need to watch the birds and see how they act after you feed a specific amount and then the next day when you fly them see and remember what they did and how they acted. If possible keep a log hanging near your kit boxes so you can make note of these changes after feeding a specific amount of feed.

I am not as strict with the feed on the young birds as I am on a hold over kit in terms of feeding. The young birds need to stay healthy and build muscle so when they start to spin they have plenty of muscle and strength to keep up the rolling often. Strong healthy birds will also tend to spin with better quality then starved birds which you will find will tend to be "sloppy" in the roll. There is really an ideal condition between starving and overfed that you are aiming for. This is a place where birds will do their optimal performing and it's up to you to find this amount of feed and exercise that will keep them at this place.

I personally find that I balance the hold over kit with a combination of proper feed and rest to find this healthy medium. This means flying one day and resting the next day and at times maybe even giving 2 days rest between flights. I have found that some birds roll so much and hard that they will not even feel the need to eat the proper amount of feed daily so rest is the only thing that will counter them falling apart on you and going light and possibly rolling down due to being too thin and weak. It's your job to watch them closely so you can prevent things like this from happening and to me rest seems to do the job on birds that over work and do not eat properly due to exhaustion mostly I think?

Again this is all part of managing your kit and if you have too many birds to manage properly you will need see things like this so you really need to find out what number of kit birds you are able to manage properly to insure they all get a fair shot at becoming good spinners. The old saying goes "if you cull a bird you can't bring it back to life…" so if this means if you manage the birds properly you will minimize culling and maximize performance of the birds you can manage properly. I can't tell you what you can manage and can't manage.

In my own case I find that about all I can manage properly is 1 hold over kit and maybe 2-3 young bird kits. If I keep more than this I tend to cull too much as I have the lack of patience for the birds and become more of a JOB to me. If all goes well I should be keeping over 1 hold over kit and 1 yearling kit each year so this means only needing to breed 50-60 babies after I reach this point each year. This is the most I can properly manage and still survive enough birds to remain hold overs each year. I have to deal with the BOP here and they take a fair share of my birds, usually around 50% of what I breed each year, but these predators have a harder time catching the mature birds and tend to get the younger birds more often. Let's not forget of course the hard working birds that can be very tired after flying and rolling for 20-30 minutes and become an easier target as well.

Here are some other information to help you analyze things more accurately in our feeds;

Protein: The protein is made up of amino acids the will help keep muscles strong and fatty acids are also part of this

Fat: Fat is obviously a way the body stores energy for the body.

Carbohydrates: There are two types of carbs we use; simple and complex. This is fast energy for our birds. This is what long distance runners strive for and these also work for our rollers.

Here is nutritional contents we see in our grains;

Grain	Protein	Carbs	Fat
Wheat	15.2%	70.9%	1.8%
Milo	11.2%	71.1%	2.9%
Safflower	9%	3%	16%
Popcorn	13.7%	66%	3.5%
Peas	22-24%	59.1%	0.9%
Vetch	20%	55.8%	17%
Barley	10.4%	66.6%	1.8%
Flaxseed	25.2%	57.8%	1.1%
Rapeseed (canola)	19.4%	16.4%	38.5%
Sunflower	14.2%	42.6%	32.3%
Millet	11.6%	67%	4%

Amino/Fatty Acids; have varying percentages of these amino acids in each grain type

Wheat/Milo/Corn/Millet - lysine, threonine, phenylalanine, isoleucine, valine, histidine, glutamic acid, proline, glycine, alanine, and cysteine

Peas – Arginine, Histidine, Isoleucine, Leucine, Lysine, Methionine, Cystine, Phenylalanine + Tyrosine, Threonine, Tryptophan, Valine

Safflower – Histidine, Isoleucine, Leucine, Lysine, Methionine, Phenylalanine, Threonine, Tryptophan, Valine

Barley – Tryptophan, Threonine, Isoleucine, Lysine, Methionine, Cystine, Phenylalanine, Tyrosine, Valine, Arginine, Histidine, Alanine, Aspartic acid, Glutamic acid, Glycine, Proline, Serine, Hydroxyproline

Sunflower – Tryptophan, Threonine, Isoleucine, Leucine, Lysine, Methionine, Cystine, Phenylalanine, Tyrosine, Valine, Arginine, Histidine, Alanine, Aspartic acid, Glutamic acid, Glycine, Proline, Serine, Hydroxyproline

As you can see many of the grains have similar amino acids but it's the percentages of these that is the difference from grain to grains. Wheat, Milo, Popcorn and Millet all have similar percentages of these acids shown.

Well I hope this article gave you some insight on the fundamentals of feeding our rollers properly and I would enjoy hearing from you on what you think and do in your own loft. Send correspondence to me at davesrollerpigeons@gmail.com

Facts sites from below sites;

http://nutritiondata.self.com/facts/
http://www.aaccnet.org/publications/cc/backissues/1971/Documents/chem48_690.pdf

***This is certainly a very important reprint here I located in some old pigeon documents I have had going back to the late 1980's. Not sure exactly where it came from but I found it in an envelope from the late Paul Bradford. I think you all will enjoy this interview done of Bill Pensom in 1963. I think you will enjoy this one.**

Questions and Answers
By
Bill Pensom
(1963)

Bruce Cooper wrote an article after Bill Pensom visited the Northwest back in Novemeber of 1963 and after Cooper visited Pensom in California. The following is Bruce Cooper's compilation of the questions he put to Bill Pensom and the answers that Pensom gave to him during their discussion.

Pensom shown here judging a show in this picture

BC: If you put it into percentages, what percent would you count for the following qualities: flying, rolling, depth, rolling quality, type and eye?

BP: Ignore depth, pick a rich eye, white, yellow or orange. Good cocks are rare: breed for rounds of young per year per pair.

BC: How important is size in a mating? Do you ever use a large bird if he is of the right type?

BP: Never use large birds. Big pigeons handle like big pigeons (I asked Pensom to show me a pigeon he would call large. He said had NONE. By the standard, I have none to large in 1963)

BC: What is the makeup of a good eye? What does placement of the pupil mean in relation to the roll?

BP: Nothing at all. Rolldowns are not detected by the pupil placement – only by the expression of the bird can you discover the rolldown. A bird can have an out-of-round pupil and not be a rolldown, or the pupil can be in the front corner of the eye and the bird can still be a very sound roller.

BC: How important is good feathering – width, back covering etc…

BP: More feather means more seldom rolling. Medium feather is the best, and the most champion performers are this way. A little lack of feather is better that too much. Only Tipplers and Racing Homers require a wealth in feather. Feather in the birds today is no problem – more have enough.

BC: Is the bird that never caused any problem, such as rolling to deep, too frequent, etc... even during the moult, much better for stock than the bird that turns out to be just a good spinner – or even a champion – but caused problems early in the kit and had to be locked up for one reason or another during his young bird training period?

BP: The True champion will fly right any time. He will never cause problems as a young bird or old bird. But a bird that you must take special precautions for can still be a valuable stock bird. The "no problem" birds breed their kind, so they are the best.

BC: Do feather-footed birds show any different traits than the clean-legged birds?

BP: Do feather-footed birds show any different traits than the clean-legged birds?

BC: of what value is a bird that was sound when you looked at him for stock, but when the breeding season is over he will not go back to the kit due to excessive rolling?

BP: If the bird was true once, he will be true again. It can take up to 18 months to find out. The question is, was he ever really a true roller?

BC: What percentage of good young birds should good stock birds produce?

BP: Seventy percent. Each pair should produce at least one really good bird each year.

BC: When do you recommend the use of a darkened kit loft? All of the time or part of the time?

BP: All of the time, but after they fly leave it light for the rest of the day.

BC: In an ideal kit, to display maximum performance, how many birds should be deep, medium and short rollers?

BP: 18 deep ones and the rest can be anything that will work frequently.

BC: How long should a champion kit fly?

BP: 35-45 minutes. A good kit should not be seen through when doing their turn.

BC: Are good birds today smaller than they were 30 years ago? If not, why not?

BP: No. You cannot get them any smaller and retain the birds. However, you must continue to breed them smaller to retain the present size. Breed as small as you can and still maintain the sound spinning qualities. Breed to obtain high velocity. The small birds can do it best.

BC: What does eye color indicate as to what sort of rolling you can expect from the pigeon?

BP: Orange or yellow eyed birds are the deepest and most frequent spinners. White and pearl eyed birds are the soundest spinners. White eyed birds are the flyers in the breed of pigeons – Tipplers, Tumblers, Cumulets, etc...

BC: How important is body length? Is it better to be small, but not too long or well-porportioned, but large?

BP: Very little importance. However, don't make a practice of breeding them too long. You must make no compromise in the quality of the spin, but you can in body length.

BC: How many year do you need to fly a pigeon – barring accidents – to prove him to be sound?

BP: 18 months. After 18 months, they should last until they are 10 years old. There is exceptions to this, but this is the general rule.

Bill said, "Don't compromise. Don't put a good one to a bad one hoping to improve the offspring. You can't breed to close if you need to find a good mate.

BC: Out of 50 young birds, how many would be expected normally to roll down today?

BP: one or two is tolerable. In the old Black Country days, half would roll down.

BC: Are birds that are in the hands of the top Roller breeders of today breeding a greater percentage of champions than they did 30 years ago?

BP: Yes. The reason is due to better education, better literature, and more communication between breeders exchanging ideas. Bill Said "Mate your birds on the ground to character, not show quality. Keep them small and closely related. The birds must have an alert look to them with a bright, all-seeing shining eye. They often have a "go-to-hell" look in the eye. Racing Homer eyesign means nothing in rollers.

BC: Do the best spinners come out of the roll in the opposite direction to that in which they were flying when they went into the spin?

BP: Yes, but very rarely do I see it and it does not mean they fly away in the opposite direction, only on the occasion do they fly out away from the kit. They change very fast and the best return to the kit formation quickly.

BC: Of what value is a pigeon that never rolls in their first three years of flying?

BP: This birds can still be a good one if it is bred off of spinners and it has the character and type. All birds must be bred to one ideal – that of high velocity spinning. A bird of good stock may possess the character and expression, but never roll itself. Very few men can see the expression. The bird must be of ideal type if he is a nonperformer after three years and only if he is bred out of the best possible stock.

BC: How do you rate the effectiveness of flying birds in an old bird flying kit?

BP: Flown mixes is best. Flown mixed, but housed separately by sex is not as good. Flown separately by sex and housed separately by sex is very poor. The pigeons do their potential best only when they are housed and flown mixed.

Bill says the birds will be only as good as the man who mated them.

BC: What do you look for in the eye of a Roller which has just flown as a sign of the pigeon's performance?

BP: Nothing is particular. I don't think this will show anything that couldn't have been told before hand.

BC: Should the rump be wide and thick or should it be narrow?

BP: It makes no difference to the spin. It should be narrow for show purposes. The keel need not be tight into the vents – only the angle of the keel going from the front to the vent is important because this makes the apple-shaped body.

BC: What is the value to the roll of the skull- frontal, back-skull and flat-headedness?

BP: None.   This is for showing purposes only. (However, Bill later told me to never use a snipey-headed bird for stock as they seldom have the expression needed).

BC: Is there any shape which is not tolerable in relation to the roll?

BP: None. Pick a uniform bird – that is all.

BC: What does the apple body feel like and look like?

BP: Too deep or too shallow is bad; the pear shape is too long. Put a head and a tail on an apple and slice off the top and you will have the apple-shaped body.

BC: How high do you call too high to fly?

BP: Out of sight. They should fly low enough that you can see them work, but high enough that they don't drop down too low when working hard. (I asked Bill if his bird were too high when they were what I would call almost too high. He said, "No, they are just right.") You judge the quality of the roll when they are down low, but when flying a kit for someone, they should be too high to tell if they are rolling right or not.   They show their best when up high and working very frequent and deep. This has nothing to do with selecting champions, but for flying a kit only. It is easy to fly a champion, but takes some ability to fly a real kit.

BC: How long do you fly young birds – in the summer and in the fall, and as old birds?

BP: As long as they want to fly in the summer. It is good for them as old birds to cut them down to 45 minutes.

BC: Does the bird that flys with his feet out when low or just after it's rolled indicate anything in particular?

BP: If the bird is safe when flying with the kit, it means nothing, except that he has probably bumped into the trees or into some other bird when in flight.

Robert Rives' Ghetto Rollers

Here's a great cock bird owned by Eric Laidler of Denmark

My old friend and 2 time National Champion Rodman Pasco of Hawaii, 2009 and 2015

Taken June 13th, 2016 at the World Cup Finals in the Redding area, unfortunately Robert's kit DQ'd on him

Left to Right; John Leake, Roxanne, Eric Duren, Danny Duren, Ferrel Bussing, Robert Anguiano, Robert Rives, Bonnie Anguiano, Fred Boyer, Michael Morris and Dave Henderson

Creating a Cross with Success
By
Dave Henderson

Crossing various lines of rollers is nothing new to most of us. Many may not even realize that there are so many specific lines or "families" of rollers out there, bred for specific reasons and developed from some select individuals that makes that flock unique to others even if they are directly related. These birds become what we have made them as pigeon breeders. These endeavors can be very rewarding or even disastrous, but the term is "live and learn". We never know how things will go until you try. Even full siblings will not produce the same, and this is the real differences that many of us fail to recognize, just the same as maybe your very best spinner may not have the ability to replicate itself and yes a lower quality siblings might have this ability to produce better than what you see in specific birds.

Many times "better" is also a misconception as what it really key is the prepotency of the bird or its ability to reproduce a high percentage of good birds on multiple mates, not necessarily better than what you are seeing. Generally speaking what you see is what you get in terms of overall quality in the roll. Very few will produce birds that are better than the qualities you see in the parents, if you flew them. The only way to find out is to put some birds together and see what you get and if you are lucky enough to find a prepotent bird then you are onto something. I think this is the "gene" you are really trying to harness in your' genepool.

You can take your time with this or you can be very progressive. What I mean by this is that if you want to allow specific birds to be paired on several mates before you assess their value (2-3 seasons) that is fine or you can put a bird on to a specific mate. I have seen many that are kind of 1 and done however, where if they don't get even descent results in the first season they discard the bird, this is up to you. A common failure of this is breeding a bird and then re-flying the bird before you are able to assess the abilities of the babies and you can lose great bird to a predator before you are even able to properly evaluate the pair itself if you are not careful. I personally like to keep a bird for 2-3 seasons before assessing its value. If you don't have room you can always have a friend use the bird at this place and see if it can produce on something.

I especially find it educational to experiment with crosses like this in an attempt to create better performing rollers, extraordinary birds. I cannot attest to what all breeders do, but I personally strive to improve my birds continually year after year and you can only do this by keeping track of the birds you produce with written records. These would include breeding records where each birds came from and then what happened to these specific birds; did you stock it, cull it, did they mysteriously vanish or where they a causality of the BOP. This is the minimum record keeping you should keep I like to rate my overall feel of specific birds to include; body type, temperament and of course all aspect of their performance. This would occur with the birds that I elect to try in the stock loft. This would include kitting, velocity, style, depth etc... If you are reluctant to experiment from time to time by crossing then you are kind of limiting your knowledge with your birds or your experience that is. There is some valuable education in this process.

There are some that have been able to develop their own lines thru a process of crossing much like what is discussed in this article. Success will vary from loft to loft and many will need further experience or even advice/education to get a better understanding of how to make crosses that you think will be successful. Anyone can toss birds in a cage and breed babies. It's not difficult but you must keep good records and be diligent in progressing forward, pay attention to the small details of these bird. You will no doubt have to cull a lot of birds before you can move forward with specific birds but it will happen if you want it to. High velocity stable birds that execute properly is the key.

Now let's discuss a little about Inbreeding and Line breeding which I think can assist you with this endeavor.

I personally don't like to practice a lot of close inbreeding in my loft but many do and have great success with it. The main reason I don't do it as I don't see the real need for it, but I might practice it more in the future and see what happens and of course document the outcome. I don't think generation after generation of full sibling matings are needed. I can see trying to breed back to one parent or anther but full siblings are not that appealing to me. I would inbred 1 generation and then line breed 3-4 generations after that, and you can go many years with only 3-4 generations even if your birds are closely related.

I think with a more line bred family I can see where it can work effectively, but what I fear in the process is what you can't see and how these characteristics affect the birds in hand, the doubling of some genes that you don't want to double up. This could be more subtle things you might not see as clearly; like the immune system for one. Inbreeding can cause weakened immune systems where you start to get a lot of birds getting sick and it's a reoccurring thing, you might find yourself constantly medicating birds to keep them healthy. This would be a big red flag that you really need to do something different to counter this affect, but in the same breath if you eliminate the birds that are showing these signs and refrain from using them in stock loft you could also strengthen your line at the same time... so it's kind of a dual edge sword with inbreeding. On one side you are eliminating the weak birds and on the other side only keeping the strong birds, but what if half of what you produce is weak and the other half strong continually? Is this type of system worth it in the long run?

I think the argument is this, if you over time eliminate the weak ones your gene pool will gradually eradicate the weak birds and breeding from only "perfect" birds will keep your line from seeing defects such as this? Well it's been my experience that these weak birds will continue to pop up often in this process and as the genetics are set in your family these characteristics are also set. This is why I suggest doing a lot less inbreeding and more line breeding is best. This would be breeding cousins, aunt to nephews, grand kids to grandparents etc...

Real inbreeding will really speed up a process that can occur in all live stock called "Inbred Depression". What is mentioned in the above paragraph is certainly related to this depression. This depression can occur with all poultry and birds when doing a lot of inbreeding. Of course depending how much inbreeding you do will vary from loft to loft and there is no way of really knowing when these negative effects (depression) will show up in your family of birds.

This depression can come in many forms from; poor hatchability of eggs and even fertility issues, mentally not normal birds, poor homing instincts and the list goes on. Generally speaking many of these will be culled on their own, but at times some showing minor issues like this can get by without you really ever fully aware of it. There is also no way of knowing when your family of birds will start showing these negative signs, whether it's 15 years, 20 years or more...

I think you can work a cousin lines and line breed them with a lot of success, without ever doing a lot of inbreeding in a system I have used that has been called Pretzel Breeding. Imagine the shape of a Pretzel, round but it crosses at the center. So the real idea here is to breed lines that are made up of related birds and then after 3-4 generations of line breeding in a specific direction (a line) you then cross these lines over to the other lines you have created and then go back out to its specific line again for another 3-4 generations (or less) back to the regular line and so forth. It's basically a system of line breeding in a loft that has all related birds from the same source this is a way to minimize the bad traits that can come from close inbreeding. It almost acts like an "out cross" at times when you cross back related birds after 3-4 generations of not being in the line. It's much simpler then you might think but you have to keep records.

I think the biggest thing you need to remember is that the greatest influences genetically are from the parents of specific birds and grandparents, but beyond that the only things that show up are usually color, patterns and body type that is passed along. Granted when line breeding it is the hope that you are able to harness specific genetics and pass these traits along to generation after generation, so to that respect you see similarities in newer generations even past grandparents. I think this is why in line breeding you can go 3-4 generations in one direction and then cross back over on distant cousin lines that also went in their own direction and have success with it, this is the fundamentals behind Pretzel Breeding.

Inbreeding pigeons is not the same as it is in humans. Pigeon have 40 pairs of chromosomes to 32 pairs in humans. Pigeons also have a higher rate of mutations within a specific genepool than do humans. So I think Mother Nature has designed our rollers with the ability to inbreed with less problems in a flock before the ill effects of "inbreeding depression" will show up. I think that most birds migrating also plays into this idea as when many birds migrate to some degree they have the ability to introduce "new blood" into their flock.

Well now that we have some basic knowledge of how to breed birds the birds and some things to avoid let's get back to the heart of this article, Creating a Cross with Success.

Well the above should give you some basic ideas on where to go with such a cross. The first obvious choice is to locate a fancier that has been breeding his line of birds for an extended period of time and is successful with them.

It would be ideal if this source also shared some related back ground of your genepool as well, best case scenario these birds came from your own loft many years earlier.

As a good rule of thumb if you are unable to locate some birds from your own line that have been bred for performance only then you need to dig deeper. You could maybe look at some of the genetics behind your birds originally and then approach an out cross in that fashion. You will not know what is available until you are able to familiarize yourself with fanciers that are currently flying rollers successfully today out there. Contact them and ask them about their birds. Find out what the genetic make-up of their birds is etc… After you are able to find some birds that fit the bill try to make a trip to see these birds in the air to better assess them. If you are unable see the birds first hand try to see if this breeder would be willing to trade some of your babies for some of theirs so you can fly them out and get your own impression of them. You have to remember that you don't need a lot of birds for this just a few select birds, even 1 good bird is all you need.

Here is a close up head shot of a SA cross

So again for me your first choice would be going to someone reputable and has breed a line of good spinners from a similar source. This would ideally be from a person or person's you possibly assisted with birds earlier and kept performance as their main concern even if these birds are not have been crossed by them. The genes are no longer the same as you have but distantly related and it's with these type of birds that you will find success generally speaking.

If you look for birds that are not related to your own look for bird that handle and fly the same as your birds do. This is feeding them similar, their mannerism and type of bird is similar to yours. These birds share primary characteristics to yours in terms of flying, feeding, mannerism and spinning. If you are generally happy with your rollers in terms of type and other qualities I would suggest looking for a cock to outcross with as I find that hens tend to be slightly dominate in terms of type when breeding so by using a cock you will continue to have birds more similar to your own birds with this cross.

The foundation of my original family 1990, ½ OD Harris ½ Paul Bradford and a little bit of Norm Reed that I am still breeding and flying today

Once you have obtained a bird that you feel is worthy of experimenting with then you will have to put this bird or birds to work. You would ideally start putting this bird on the best stock birds you have of the opposite sex. You will want to breed as many birds from this outcross and then continue to move the bird around on other suitable mates over the next several years. I would think by the second or third year of doing this you would have been able to assess if this pigeon is going to work for you. Ideally you will see results in the first season but this is not always the case so be persistent and properly assess these birds over time. Don't be hasty and try to envision a long term goal for this cross and what your goals are for doing it. If the bird does not work you can maybe offer it back to the breeder and maybe try another one from this breeder, or not this is up to you.

The quality that many are looking for with crosses is something called "Hybrid Vigor". The Racing Pigeon sport has been practicing this for a very long time and this is something most are well aware of. This basically means that when you cross two long bred "real" families together there is a tendency to produce some exceptional pigeons in the original crossing. You want to be able to harness these qualities and develop them into a working line of pigeons, but many have no desire to do this and only use these pigeons to compete with. I think that why not try to work these birds into their own line, creating a 3ʳᵈ line (or more). If it works it could change everything but it doesn't work then it's easy enough to fix, you cull them and forget you ever did it.

This is why I think its import to run lines in your loft and not have everything in one basket so to speak. If everything is the same and you eventually run into a "wall" then there is no way to fix it, but if you keep these lines separate and move forward with them you can always start over at some point. So be aware that some lines might be slightly better than others but it's with the balance of both that you are able to keep the line strong and prolific.

New subline project, one of my old line hens X to pure South African cock

Well this will conclude this article but I hope that you get some good insight or at least ideas that can better assist you with your own birds. Please feel free to contact me if you want to better understand things at davesrollerpigeons@gmail.com.

The Modoc High Mountain Futurity Fly got underway and Danny Duren and family are very excited to bring this event to the participants. The event was opened up to 80 birds this year and only 30 were taken in. Danny Duren and family are so confident that this will be such a great event for the fanciers flying that he is donating the feed to take care of these birds throughout the 12 months this event will take place.

Here is the payout for the season;

1st $350 + Plague (7x9)
2nd $175 + Plague (6x8)
3rd $125 + Plague (5x7)
4th $100 prize
5th $75 prize
Loft Managers Choice – Plague (5x7) +$50
Best Deep Spinner – Plague (5x7) +50
The breeders that will be given back ½ the selling price of each surviving bird unless breeder says otherwise (after auction fees)

The Futurity Kit box for the 30 entries this season

In The Spotlight

Interviews in the hobby

***Alan is an incredible roller flyer living in the UK. He has a proven track record in the roller circuit going back 20+ years. I hope you enjoy what he has to say.

Meet Alan Milne UK

Name, age, where do you live; describe your location in the UK (east side, south etc...) and the various climates there where you live

Alan Milne I am 53 years old. I live in the North Eastern region in England. The climate is kind of erratic where I live, it is windy a lot and the weather can change very quickly. The winters are very cold and we can easily see negative degree weather here. I usually pair up my pigeons in December and breed until around May each year.

How long have you been working with your current family of rollers and what various families of birds or bloodlines are behind them?

I have had this blood line about 20+ years now and the birds originate from Middlesbrough through Peter Harper and Les Bezance. These two lines were crossed together to make my current family of rollers.

You mentioned that you have birds from Harper and Bezance? Do you have any other blood lines in your loft currently? You never tried birds from Morris Hole?

I have never tried birds from Morris Hole, I don't have any other bloodlines in my family of birds.

Alan with Heine Bijker during World Cup Finals

How many birds are behind the gene pool you are currently using? Do you continue to add in birds from Peter and Les or just got some originally (what year?) and are still working with them? Please give details on the background of your birds if you can.

I am currently still breeding from my family of birds. I first started off with 1 cock bird I borrowed from Les and then obtain 2 other Bezance birds from another source and bred them together. I got a few others from Peter Harper and ended up crossing these together and formed a great family that I still fly today. I don't have any original birds left from Peter or Les but I can go right back to the pedigrees I have kept. I have a record stock book which I write everything down and I can go back to 1992.

What was the first good spinning/breaking kit you can remember, and who owned this kit?

The first good kit of birds I ever seen spinning with good quality were in Middlesbrough, England. These birds were flown by Steve Dixon and were all black and white balds. These birds balled up tight every one of them it was quite a site. If I recall correctly I think he was flying in the nationals that day. I recall that Graham Dexter was juding this kit and they were very active. Unfortunately a couple of the birds came down early which gave him a DQ, but in my eyes this was the best kit I have seen and now I hold this standard for my own birds even today. Once you see a kit like this you never forget it.

Here is on of Alan's stock pairs

What do you think of the general overall quality of the BR today (2015) and how was it different when you first started with rollers? Did you ever get any insight on the rollers in the early days in your region?

I think rollers are getting better now there is still some good quality rollers about now. When I started keeping rollers over 20 years ago it was hard to get good stock birds as we didn't have a club at the time were I live and if any one got good birds were you lived they kept them for themselves good rollers were worth their weight in gold to get any of these great rollers. A few of us started visiting pigeon breeders and shows and this was where I met George Kitson from Middlebrough, this was around 1990.   George was the one that introduced us to the other Middlesbrough fanciers. There were many good flyers at this time and I began visiting as often as I could. I only lived 35 miles away at the time.

What has been the best recent kit(s) you have seen? How did these stand out? (say top 5 in recent years)

Peter Harper flew a good kit of young birds that stood out a few years back and flew well in a gusty wind worked well as a team. His kit flew in a very tight pattern and were breaking with some nice depth in the 25 foot range. This was a young bird team.

Eddy Baldwin flew a good yearling kit which stood out well putting in some big breaks with good quality and depth. His kit was knocking of 25-30 foot breaks in a very impressive fashion. This kit faltered a few times but it's the quality deep breaks that really stand out to me. This was during the All England Roller Club fly.

What club(s) do you fly with and how many flyers are in these clubs you compete with?

At the moment I am in three clubs my local club which is the, Tyne and Wear Roller Club (TWRC) and has 18 members. I am also in the City of Sunderland Roller Club (COSRC) which has about 19 members, and I am in one of the biggest clubs in England which is the, All England Roller Club (AERC) which has a several hundred members and has a large flies each year. They fly young birds, yearlings and old birds.

The All England Roller Club holds a series of flies each year for old birds, young birds and yearlings. The yearling competition must have been banded with birds all from the previous year. The competition can be broken into several contests at the same time which includes the Aggregate Trophy, Merit Trophy and Rose Bowl Winner.

We have the Aggregate Trophy that is combining the totals from the Old Bird and Young Bird and there is the Rose Bowl Winner that is awarded to the Best Overall Spinner displayed across all kits that flew in the AERC flies.

The Merit Trophy is the kit that was awarded the highest amount of quality points in the AERC Fly.

The Pensom Shield Trophy is the award given to the AERC's best Young bird kit that was flown off against the best Young birds team from the Midland Roller Pigeon Club. The kit that wins this fly off wins the Pensom Shield.

If you could just name 1 person of interest that has influenced you the most over the years with the BR, who would this person be and why?

It would have to that Peter Harper that has influenced me the most over the years. Peter doesn't fly rollers much these days but still helps people out with birds and there are a lot of people flying his birds going back to the 1990's. Many fanciers have done well flying birds from Peter over the years.

Many of my first mentors were lads from Middlesbrough. I would go down and watch their birds fly and go round as many flys. I then I had a good idea what I was wanting to breed for. There was another lad that flew birds from

Morris Hole from Shildon that I could visit often. As I mentioned Peter Harper, Les Bezance and George Kitson were all lads I liked to go watch their birds fly.

How many stock birds do you breed from on average each season? How many babies do you produce on average? Do you use foster parents, full time or part time?

I will normally pair up 16 pairs each season of 6-8 are stock pairs and the rest are experimental pairs. I don't normally use any foster pairs and I will normally breed 80 birds per year.

A couple pairs of Alan's birds in their boxes

Describe the environment in your breeding loft, and your goals from your stock birds in the coming year?

I have 8 nest boxes in each breeding section with a small wire mesh pen on the front of my shed where they can have a bath regularly. My goal every year is to win with my young birds and win the All England Young Bird Fly which I have been second and third many times. My breeding sections are 4ft x 8ft and I feed and water these birds colony style.

The front of Alan's loft

What was the best bird you have ever seen flown? Describe its characteristics and qualities.

The best bird I've seen roll was a checker white bald hen which I have in stock now it rolls about 25 feet balled up nice and tight and goes straight back to the kit every time it rolls. This bird was flawless as a young bird and was abnormally frequent.

What has been your best stock birds in your own family? (Attach pic if possible) Describe their characteristics

I have about 4 really good stock pairs in my loft. These pairs produce very good young in high percentages. The birds they produce are the type of rollers I like; fast spinners that kit exceptionally.

What would you say are the most important qualities in selecting a good solid stock bird? (Please rank these qualities by their importance to you)

I look for birds that have NO faults and will not breed from a roller until it is at least 2 years old. The roller must have very good quality spin and ball up tight and go straight back to the kit after it rolls.

If you could pick one region (club) in the UK that possessed more good kits from top to bottom which club or region would this be in your opinion? Who are the top flyers in this region?

I would have to say the North Eastern side of England has some very good flyers. We have Deano Forester, Keith Storey, Eddy Baldwin, yours truly, Ross Young, John Hall, Colin Bailey, Andy Dawson, the late Morris Hole, Peter Harper and Les Bezance. As you can see this is a very competitive group of flyers that have put up some fantastic kits in the World Cup over the years.

What advice would you give to any would be roller flyer that is open minded out there wanting to fly in better rollers?

I would tell any new flyers to go and visit as many lofts and see as many kits as they can. Talk to fanciers and see them yourself so that you are able to assess what type of performance you are after in this hobby. These new guys should keep their gathering of rollers to a minimum as it's too easy to get too many different kinds of birds. If you want to do well don't keep more than two different families in the same loft. I think this is the best when starting out so that you are able to stay focused on developing a good performance line of birds.

Getting off to a Great Start with Young Birds
By
Camillo Paci

Over the past few years I have heard of the troubles some have training new rollers and some of the losses they sustain in this process. Losing youngsters and poor trapping issues seem to be common occurrences with many roller fanciers, and I wanted to share some of my thoughts and observations on the subject. I haven't flown off a young bird in many, many years, and when I did it was entirely my fault. As a young man I had plenty of time on my hands. So much of that time was spent in my yard with my birds. I quickly learned that there are no substitutes for careful attention and time investment.

One of the most important factors in training young birds is time. To correctly get young birds on the wing and reinforce the best flying and trapping habits, you have to invest the time to do it right. It is not something you can do on your lunch break or before a family outing. You have to clear your schedule for the day, and be sure to let everyone know you have set the day aside to train your birds. Stepping away for just a few moments can result in a loss. As a trainer, you have to be ready for any possible event, not matter how unlikely it may occur. Young birds can do weird things, putting them in and out of view on the roof line, so be ready at all times. I think training youngsters is like herding sheep, in that you are close by and know where the birds are at all times. You certainly wouldn't leave them to graze on a hillside and go shopping for the day. I find myself constantly counting them as they drop in and out of view, even for just a few moments. Being attentive to your birds is very important not just for what they are doing, but what could enter their space to frighten them as well.

Camillo's kit boxes

Depending on the time of year, a youngster could be snatched off by a Cooper Hawk without anyone even noticing it at all. Even the mere presence of the handler could be enough to deter a hawk from making a more brazen attack. If you have pets, keep them indoors. I have young children that love to scare the birds up. They are very helpful in releasing the older kits, but could scare the young ones off very easily. Once the birds become familiar with their surroundings, you can then introduce pets and family members.

I like to fly English style, to get the most control over my birds. One would think that training birds through a big wide open door would be more difficult than trapping birds thru wire traps or a drop style door, but it simply isn't so. I do however recommend installing a drop or trap style entrance on the kit boxes at the top for those times when you might have to leave the yard in an emergency, or the pigeon simply get out of the loft. They are great to have, but should not be your main option.

The young birds being called in to the feeding pan

One of the biggest mistakes people make is not weaning the youngsters soon enough. The connection the youngsters have with their parents should shift immediately to the handler when you wean them. You should wean them when they begin to pick grain by themselves and I find this is best time to pull them. The hunger and excitement works to your advantage when they are in the kit box. The frenzy is an invaluable tool the first few days when they join the kit box which helps them establish control very quickly. As a general rule, squeakers should be pulled just before the feathers are completely filled in under the wings. Even sooner, if the birds are beginning to pick grains along with the parents. Keep a close watch on their habits as they approach the first 24-26 days of life. Pulling the birds too late means you could be working with birds that are too far developed and too strong on the wing. This can be disastrous, as they could fly to high for their own good, unable to find their way back. The earlier you wean them, the more trust you will gain from the birds.

Training young birds is all about control. It is also so with the older birds, but it's never more important than it is when you are establishing a connection with them in the very beginning. The key to control is feed. It is as simple as that. Once they recognize you are the source of their food, you are ready to train them. One of the things you should consider is the method of grain distribution. I like to use a large metal baking pan (tray). I have found that the sound it makes when the grain is dropped in this pan and the other pecking sounds from the birds' beaks makes these trays a valuable tool. It also spreads the grain out nicely so that no single birds are getting too much and others not enough feed. I also like to use the bakers' cup, or an aluminum can/cup to rattle the feed. Some prefer to whistle, but I much prefer the can. I find it easier to call them down by rattling some loose grain in it that has a very distinct sound, but a visual if the birds are still flying about the loft. Whatever your technique is to call the birds back to the feed will work and you should only pick one method and never change.

I have found that a lot of the kit box designs or techniques revolve around convenience. Although some of these ideas can be clever, they detract from the time investment of the handler. Kit box sun cages, traps and all these things I see as things that can make the handler lose focus of what is most important. I would rather have my birds' sun on the loft on their own, not in a cage. I also don't train my birds to use the traps until they are kitting well and are beginning to make their first somersaults.

My goal in the first 2 days of training is to get the youngsters to react to the feed can, by having them exit the kit box, immediately hitting the roof of the kit box, and then all completely trapping back in at my command in less than 10 seconds. If the birds are young, hungry and have shown they are reacting to the handler, this can be easily accomplished. I generally let the youngsters come out on the first day on their own. I let them check out their surroundings and find their way to the top of the kit box. They are not extremely hungry at this point, but they are just hungry enough that they will trap back into the open door just below them when I toss some grains on to the feed pan. They are not afraid of my hands or arms, or my very presence in general. They will often land on my shoulders or hands to chase the grain. This is an important bond we gain with these youngsters. They will undoubtedly trap in with ease when they are this comfortable. I usually only give them just a few grains each, and repeat the process over and over for most of the day. I usually time my releases every 15 minutes or so. The more times they trap the fuller they will become and react slower to the feed can. If I notice they are not trapping quickly on the releases, I lengthen the times between releases, and perhaps hold back the feed a bit more. We want to reinforce good habits, by having slow re-entries, we are moving backwards in the process. Always keep these youngsters on the edge the first couple of days.

Once the birds are trapping nicely on their own and reacting to the can, I will ease up just a bit on the rationing. I want them to enjoy the release and look forward to it. I encourage them to take first flights around the yard. They may get a little scared and land on the roof or the house or at the neighbor's roof, but they WILL find their way back soon enough. This part of this training is very important. Having birds that are not fully developed will ensure they don't fly too far or too high. Always keep count on the kit and make sure they trap in all together. Keep the kit box closed and when the final bird hits the rooftop, then you can open the door and allow them to trap in as a group. It is important to not trap in the first birds that land, as the stragglers will be hungry, and opening the door could risk re-releasing birds that have already eaten. You will find that birds are enjoying being out of the kit box, and the first flights are very exciting. After all, they were born to fly.

Now it is time to chase the birds up... This stage of the process can be tricky. They are now strong enough to take their flights but have to be chased up because they don't really take to the sky on their own. The longer they light on the rooftops, the more accustomed they will be to simply lounging around. It is important to begin chasing them up for the first flights, but not to truly frighten them. There should be no fear associated to the kit box or areas close to it. I see many handlers sticking flags in their kit boxes to scare them out. I prefer to open the door and let them come out on their own. Have faith in the fact that they truly desire taking to the air, they will do well. If flagging is your method to chase them up, do it when the birds are leaving the kit box. Using a standard 6 foot pole with any cloth attached to the end of it will do the trick.

The flag that is used to get them up in the air, should be one that they have never seen up to this point in their training. Considering this it will be a factor in getting them to fly higher.   Be confident in that the birds will find their way back home at this point.   They have had more than enough time to examine their surroundings and explore far enough from the loft to figure it out. Some youngsters will go missing for long periods of time.   I have often found birds like this to be just out of my sight, and are safe as can be. Once the birds have scattered and take their first flight, wait until they find the top of the kit box, and allow them to trap. Feed them as you have up until now. Again, wait until they are all together. If anything, allow for the straggler or two. It happens. They will trap after the second release. Young birds sometimes freeze on the rooftops in the neighborhood until they see more fluttering or activity from the group to find their way back.

Another common problem is with the birds trapping and feeding at different times. As I just pointed out, you will get stragglers, and late trappers during the learning process. So if there are birds that have already trapped and eaten, and birds that wish to trap and have not, what is the solution? The answer is quite simple and is important even with the older kits. When this does happen, you all have to "level them out." By this I mean all the birds have to be brought to a point of hunger/satisfaction that they will all feed the same. Fed birds will want to fly longer, and hungry birds will not want to fly as long. To correct this, you can't punish the late trappers by NOT feeding them. This may be useful for high flyers and late trapping older birds, but never with young birds just learning the ropes. Young birds usually late to trap for a reason. They either got lost, or frightened. If there are late trapping issues, I allow for the first group to trap, I feed them just enough to keep them hungry so that if the door were to re-open, they will still be in the feeding mode.   This will allow you to trap in any stragglers late while the birds can all get a full ration. I allow them to take in as much feed as they will eat. At this point, you can skip the next day feeding and they will all be on the point by the third day. Now this is in case of a messy trapping day. Usually, with most handlers, the kinds of things can be worked out more easily than having to use such measures. But this is definitely a useful tool to get the team back on the same page. Try to keep a dropper available as well to flag in stragglers. I usually use an old bird, with primaries removed. I keep the dropper hungry as well. I toss the dropper high enough to catch the stragglers attention, and the dropper is limited to simply falling to the roof and not taking flight. A confused young bird will zoom in on a dropper nicely and find its way back.

With each passing day, these youngsters will gain confidence and climb higher in to the sky. Do not expect too much of them such as kitting on the first few days. They are still learning their way around. Kitting will not happen until a few days after their first flights. Smaller groups will take longer to kit than larger groups. It just seems more natural for larger groups to fly in formation and take shape.

Now you are on your way.

Once the birds are all kitting together well, fly them twice a day for the first few weeks. This will accelerate their training and they will come into the roll faster. When you see the birds gaining strength and starting to truly flip over start to limit their releases to once per day and give them a single day of rest each week. Multiple releases are great for initial training and enforcing good habits, but it will fly the roll out of them.

So remember, you have done everything you can to get them on their way. By using the feed can and giving them close observation, you will have no issue keeping control of them.

This is one of my favorite pics showing a few of Camillo's birds, really amazing picture

Giving Iodine to our Rollers

By
Dave Henderson

This article is kind of close to home for me and I thought it might be helpful to inform others about what I have discovered in my own loft.

I have had a few of my hens that are in their prime, but have weird issues of not laying very quickly, some have even appeared to stop laying even at young ages of 6-7 years old. A few are so slow, that they will only lay again after the babies leave the nest. This is just not very productive and with other birds putting up 2-3 times the production of these "slow" layers it almost seems a waste of time to continue using them. However they are in my program for 1 reason, to quality performance so I feel almost compelled to test their genetics. These same hens always seemed to look "sickly" or get stressed easy during the breeding season, much faster than my average bird. I thought maybe that had a calcium deficiency or something similar but after doing more reading it is more likely something else is going on. Their eggs looked completely normal (no calcium issue) and have some hatchability issues as well and when you combine this with the slow laying its' something I really had not dealt with before.

I thought early on that is must be some lingering illness that had settled in the sex organs and might have caused scar tissue in the female parts or something. I have even considered it might even be a condition from too much inbreeding called "**Inbred Depression**". I know that this depression is a genetic issue and can run in specific birds that might have been too inbred over the years. The only problem is I don't do a lot of inbreeding so this is really not going to be the issue I feel. I really don't want to throw money and have the birds tested at the vets, it just doesn't seem worth it to me personally, so I continue to read about things it could be and experiment.

The condition or issues first started with 3-4 hens I got from my friend Cesar, I did not raise any of these particular birds. The first thing that came to my mind was **paratyphoid,** but the fact is less than 5% of all eggs that don't hatch is due to paratyphoid. This bacteria can get in the eggs and kill our pigeon embryos but it's just not as common as many think, even though all of our pigeons are carry the paratyphoid bacteria in them.

I did some more reading with some known pigeon vets well all know and indeed specific bacteria can settle in the sex organs and can cause issues with fertility and this seemed to be my first option. I treated with the suggested amount of doxycycline (pills per hen) that was prescribed to fix them in the off season and no change. It suggested a 15 day regimen of pills per bird and this would also cause you to also treat for yeast infections before following up with probiotics. This whole process was approximately 30 days to complete, but the issue did not go away when the breeding season started the following season.

Then this season came with one of the young hens showing similar symptoms with her 2nd clutch of eggs which did not hatch. I substituted foster eggs to them and they raised them fine. Then the 3rd set of eggs also did not hatch (more foster eggs) and the next set never came for another month, but they both came and both hatched. So this then told me that it must be something else but what, it certainly seemed like some supplemental issue to me at this point.

After trying to explore many issues in regard to fertility issues with our pigeons I felt I was getting lost and frustrated that I could not figure it out, until I recently stumbled on some literature that got my attention. This literature dealt with **poultry and pigeons** of course, but they do and can experience similar issues and most of it deals with fertility issues and the diagnosis fits the bill for **Iodine Deficiency** (goiter). I have heard about iodine being helpful to with hatchability of eggs but never really knew why this was, I never researched it more of why it worked at the time. I just assumed it was sanitizing the tissue to kill bacteria inside the pigeon or something which again seemed like it was neutralizing some bad bacteria, kind of like bleach in the water killing bad gut bacteria or apple cider vinegar.

It seemed most of the literature was centered on chickens (of course) that were slow to lay eggs (or stopped laying altogether) and also had issues with low hatchability rates. These were at farms that sell baby chickens primarily. It mentioned that due to genetics that some chickens will show problems with their thyroid which can lead to these problems, so this sort of lead me to think again "inbred depression". The simple fix it appears is to add iodine to your birds' diet and it seemed to be the simple fix. It explained that the biggest issue is usually giving an ALL grain diets to our birds as grain doesn't have a lot of iodine in it, and is not sufficient enough to fix issues that might arise and surprisingly enough mineral grit does not have iodine in it either like you might think. They talked about using either Lugol Iodine or Tincture Iodine in the water 1-2 times per week during the breeding season. If you breed in the winter it's even more needed if breeding this time of the year due to the lack of longer day lights days when natural elements can be depleted at a much faster rate. An easy to fix to this is feeding pigeon pellets to breeders.

You also need to keep the doses conservative as giving too much is worse than not enough, as it can build up toxins in their system and can kill them with no sign of even being sick, iodine is poisonous in higher doses. Iodine is also a very good disinfectant in water, which is a common quality of garlic.

I think the thing that is interesting is that all of these hens with the exception of one were directly related all to a great spinner I bred in 2006. So this tells me that just like people that specific birds could have a naturally under producing Thyroid glands. Common signs of this is overweight birds, sometime have a cough or respiratory issue, but giving antibiotics does not make it go away. The biggest issues again showing a weak or poor immune system. These are conditions that are not uncommon in our world today, so why could this not happen in our pigeons. I mean big pharma is here for similar reasons and this sort of things keeps them in business.

During the breeding season our cocks and hens deplete many of their natural elements in their bodies feeding and rearing babies. These lack of elements in the body can cause a lot of stress to the birds. The most important trace minerals that our pigeons need during the breeding season are; Iodine, Iron, Copper and Zinc and that a deficiency in any of these trace elements will cause breeding performance issues.

I even discovered that iodine can help with joint issues in our older pigeons (mounting cocks especially) and will increase their metabolism which will on its own stimulate productivity. So if you have a pair that is laying eggs and it appears the cock is not getting the job done it could very well be he needs iodine to help with flexibility in their joints and is really NOT STERILE like you might have thought. I am even considering ibuprofen to some of my older cock birds for this reason.

Here is a couple quotes written about iodine deficiency at www.merckvetmanual.com which sounds amazingly similar to what I have going on to some degree. *"The iodine content of an egg is markedly influenced by the hen's intake of iodine. Eggs from a breeder fed an iodine-deficient diet will exhibit reduced hatchability and delayed yolk sac absorption".* At www.nap.edu/read/2114/chapter/9#57 it states *"Inadequate production of thyroid hormones results in poor growth, lack of egg laying, and egg size. Iodine deficiency in breeders results in low iodine content of the egg yolk and, consequently, decreased hatchability and thyroid enlargement in the embryos".*

Iodine is also very important with feather quality and feather growth (during the molt) in our birds and the lack of luster on the feathers. So feather quality can be greatly improved with the use of iodine in the water once per week. The ingestion of excess amounts of feed containing goitrogenic agents (chemicals that interfere with the normal function of the thyroid gland) including soybean, flax and rapeseed. Several greens can also affect the thyroid such as turnips, and members of the cabbage family such as kale, cabbage, and broccoli. Much of the iodine in plants is based on the levels found in the dirt it grows in. *If you want to use natural methods of keeping iodine at healthy levels with your birds you could also use raw garlic or garlic juice in the water which will keep iodine levels healthy without any risks of toxins or accidental poisoning.*

Here are some other signs of goiter in our birds?

The thyroid gland of a bird is located in the chest cavity, when enlarged, can place pressure on the heart, digestive system, lungs, and air sacs. The pressure on the heart may also cause buildup of fluids in the respiratory system. These conditions on their own can kill our birds. Excessive fluids can also be produced in the digestive system. Signs of an enlarged thyroid in the throat:

- Seizures and or sudden death from physical compression of the heart and large blood vessels

- Difficulty swallowing
- Crop distention
- Regurgitation issues
- Obvious weight loss
- Lack of appetite due to partially blocked esophagus
- Wheezing or coughing

Clinical signs in pigeons are related to the lower than normal levels of hormone produced, resulting in:

- Immunodeficiency
- Bird is very susceptible to other infections/bacteria
- Obesity
- Poor reproduction – laying problems in hens
- Abnormal feather issues
- Lethargic and not acting normally

Suggested Doses of 2% Iodine for our birds

2 drops to a quart of fresh water or 1 teaspoon to a gallon of water once per week. This must be their only source of drinking water when given. So the basics is give it for 1 day just like other supplements and then the following day give fresh water again.

Here listed below are a couple of items I get a semi local supplier near me called Merca Systems located in Walnut Creek, CA. They specialize in pigeon medications and supplements as well as other pet products. Whenever I want something I check with these guys first as I can get stuff from them at times over night depending on what time I order it. **This company is called Merca Systems out of Walnut Creek, California**

Klaus Pico-Bird Jod-Eisen Plus, a compound rich in iron and iodine. Preventive Excellent 100% natural which also regulates metabolism. Bird cage, singing, parakeets and all parrots

INDICATIONS
- Iron to stimulate metabolism
- The iron increases the formation of red blood cells
- Improves absorption of oxygen by the blood
- Iodine to stimulate thyroid function
- Iodine is a 100% natural preventative against diseases caused by bacteria

DOSAGE:
- 10 ml (1/2 tablespoon) water for each liter

HOW TO USE:
- During breeding, 2 times a week

Beyers Looksap-Garlic Juice water soluble

DESCRIPTION:
- Water soluble concentrated garlic oil in a dextrose solution

- It combines the purifying effects of the garlic oil with the glucose providing the energy particularly recommended after race or after treatments against coccidiose or worms

HOW TO USE:
-One to two teaspoons per liter of drinking water twice a week

The products I purchased shown here with permission from Merca Systems

***As I am finishing up this article I am seeing results from the garlic and iodine supplements and even my old 10 year old hen that I thought was done laying has now laid again...

Cited

www.merckvetmanual.com/mvm/poultry/nutrition_and_management_poultry/mineral_deficiencies_in_poultry.html

orpingtonclub.proboards.com/thread/300/liquid-iodine#ixzz4AGRfE3ax

Donny James "Using Iodine in the water" NBRC May-June 2003

www.pigeons.biz/forums/f14/lugols-iodine-40623.html

www.peteducation.com/article.cfm?c=15+1829&aid=2755

Progression through Selection
By
Dave Henderson

There are some things we do as pigeon breeders that will assist us in this process and it's something we have to work at and it's thru good record keeping and proper management that we hope you can stay on a path to success. It's not going to be an easy road but I can assure you and if you are persistent and passionate enough you can accomplish nearly anything you set your mind to do in regards to flying better rollers.

In order to get moving forward we need to approach our pigeons with a scientific method. This means keeping records on the pairs, what babies come from these pairs and evaluating the outcome of these pairings. We need to both track good and bad traits in these pairs, not just the good birds. I also find it is very good information to track the various losses we experience as well. Some birds just simply learn how to survive and this is all part of this process of evaluating our birds. Keep records and never trust things to memory and the easier your system is while still remaining accurate is the path you need to follow. The more birds you breed the more data there is so this is why I suggest keeping things on a manageable scale so you don't get lost in this process, manageable to me may not be the same for you.

The whole process of progression is a normal process in life especially for the fanciers choose to raise the rollers in a way that you can be successful in the end. This is simply to do the best they can with the birds they have and to develop them to something extra ordinary. In the end, you will find that this is also going to end up being the most rewarding part of this hobby, but this is up to each individual. No one can make you follow the steps needed to be successful, you need to do this on your own. The old saying is *"You can lead a horse to water, but you can't make them drink…"* So basically what this means to a roller breeder is that you have to want to be better and do better and this process all starts with educating yourself to do what is needed for this to happen. To me there is nothing better than matching up a pair you like together, flying the young and then seeing them become good spinners that you can be proud of.

We don't progress with the usual good birds, we progress with the extra ordinary ones. The programs that are the most successful across the planet are the ones that are developed from a select number of "key" individuals. It does not happen just because you want it to, but you can get lucky from time to time. It's line breeding to key individuals that gives you the ability to progress.

The steps we take in progressing our rollers is really just a state of mind, it is like being self-motivated and having a desire to do more with these rollers and envisioning the path to get there. It's really the path to get there that can hang up many of us as we really just keep **too many pigeons.** Keeping too many pigeons is one of the worst things we can do if we want to be successful with the ones you have. What is too many pigeons? Well a good rule of thumb might be if you are able to keep track of all the birds you have, fly them with little effort and be able to manage the birds in a way that will benefit them and your program then you probably have the right number, but if you are culling birds on a whim, can't properly band and record the birds you are breeding and find errors often in your records then you probably have too many. These numbers will not be the same for all of us.

A manageable number for me is keeping 12 pairs or less, breeding and flying around 80 birds a year. The fewer I can keep and fly the better the birds generally do under my management system. I just personally don't want to make the birds a JOB that I can't escape from. I want it to be enjoyable and there is a balance to anything in life and it's finding that balance that will be the most rewarding to you.

There are many reasons why fanciers keep too many pigeons. I think firstly they feel the birds are just valuable to them and yes many of them they might have paid some good money for and just don't feel good about throwing money away. Some fanciers just like to collect birds from various families out there to say they have some, others just don't feel like they can properly assess and evaluate them until they have had them 4-5 years in their stock loft on many different mates and the list goes on. Whatever the reason is you really need to be disciplined enough to *"bite the bullet"* at times and move forward on an educated guess to simplify things in your loft. This is why we keep records.

I personally can't see myself keeping on to a pigeon for more than 3 seasons if I have not seen a fair number of good spinners come from this bird. What is a fair number? I would say at a very minimal figure would be 1 in 5 or 6 produced early on and if I am seeing multiple birds each year that are getting my attention then I might be onto something. At some point you need to analyze your situation and you only want to progress your program with birds that are extra ordinary. This also means birds that working more with birds that produce a larger percentage of good spinners in comparison to others you might have. I have personally had pairs that were so good together that they might actually produce 100% good breeder worthy spinners but I was not able to label them as such only due to some birds being lost one way or another, usually to the predators.

Well you might ask *"What is extra ordinary in comparison to your normal good spinner?"* This is a good question. I would personally say that your ordinary good spinner is something you see pretty often but is without a doubt good enough to breed from and might very well produce fantastic pigeons for you, but when you see them spin you don't look in AWE! The bird that I am talking about takes your breath away when you see it perform and will also appear to be nearly flawless in its execution EVERYTIME it spins. When we see a bird like this its burns into your memory forever. Again this caliber of this bird might not be the same for all fanciers *(especially if you have poor eye sight)* but for me this bird simply put looks like a spinning ball up there whether is shows a hole or not. These birds will perform like a *"Yoyo"* up there, they spin out fast and return to the kit faster and appear to enjoy what they are doing. They perform with such speed that it's is impossible to guess how many revolutions they do during a single spin without using high speed video. Many might even reference these birds as looking like a blur and will descend *(drop altitude)* slower than the normal roller does. Many birds of this type will rarely spin beyond 20 or 25 foot but their ability is undeniable. These same pigeons do all this and are never a problem in the kit. They kit tight, always perform in the kit and develop over time.

After breeding birds for many years you will find that breeding and having birds that are capable to reproducing good birds is the direction you need to go in. Sometimes these extra ordinary rollers fail to reproduce themselves. I find it especially beneficial to find a full siblings or even the nestmate of this extra ordinary pigeon that is also a good spinner and stock it up as well. The sibling actually might end up being the better producer for you, but you need to experiment with this in your own loft. You will discover over time that **all birds are not created equal** and you need to remember this. Successful lofts are found mostly on key individuals that we line breed with.

We can have top spinners that at times will never reproduce spinners which seems very odd to me and we can even at times have birds, for whatever reason, were not flown out that end up being some of our best producers in the stock loft. The birds either have it or they don't, this means genetically capable of replicating good spinners. This is the key to the whole equation to progression, having a line of birds that are capable to reproducing themselves.

Some might think this sounds easy enough to do and theoretically it is just like anything else, a process of progressing your birds it just takes time to find these birds. It's just easier said than done and certainly can't happen overnight miraculously just because you want it to. This whole process takes a lot of work and persistence to progress your birds, but it will happen if you want it to. Breeding rollers takes time, so you have to stay focused on specific goals to progress our birds from year to year, the word is *"Baby steps"*. This is the best we can do and if you are not in the birds for the long haul then it certainly won't happen.

Much of what we do simply is about putting in the time to discover outcomes. If we just fly the birds and never observe them while flying we are missing out on the majority of the important information we need to properly evaluate them. We need to see what their tendencies as the old saying is **"Like Breeds - Like..."** If you don't watch them during the evaluation period you are just doing things lazily which will not end well for you in the long run. We need to know the birds like the back of our hands so we can know what to expect from them in the future. Even minor developmental things will haunt you later on if you don't pay attention. This could include being too frequent, flying out of the kit too much, coming down early and the list goes on. These are serious flaws assuming that they are completely healthy while having this issues.

No doubt a big part of this will be how long it takes the birds to develop into spinners and much of this has to do with home much air time they get as very young birds. It's hard to judge the birds if the problem is dealing with you not being able to properly fly them so they are able to develop properly. Many times birds if they are not flown can even prevent them from developing altogether, especially cock birds as they will lose focus on flying and focus their attention on breeding which will force you to cull many of them. Had you flown them regularly and kept these birds on proper diet this might not have happened and thus you ended up culling a bird that may not have really been a cull at all, you just simply neglected it. The bottom line is if you can't properly fly them in the neighborhood of 5-6 days a week you will really not be able to evaluate them and progress your gene pool to the next level.

Developing the roll is almost like riding a bike, the more you practice the sooner and better you can do it. Over time it will even become a 2nd nature to you and this is the same for our rollers. This is not to think there will not be any mistakes along the way, we just hope these mistakes don't cull them at the same time – via bumping or rolling into hard objects. All these facets play into our bird development even your work schedule.

Considering all the above you might even need to evaluate what family of birds have work with even. If you can only get birds out 3-4 days a week regularly birds that might take 5-6 months to develop under normal daily conditions might take a year or more and like I mentioned many may not even develop properly causing you to cull them. So you might be better off finding some of the 3-4 month developers that might develop within 6 months with minimal flying. No matter what you decide to do or breed the birds will all eventually develop the way you have made and selected them over time. So someday down the road if your schedule changes and you are able to fly the birds more you will again run in to development issues and have to alter things all over again. It's just the nature of things.

I talked with Jerry Higgins after he retired and he was experiencing much of what I mention above. He went from flying 4 days a week to flying 7 days a week and this played a huge part in how the bird developed. He told me more of the birds began to get too hot with more flying and this caused him to change his game plan. So as I mentioned your schedule plays a big part in the birds' development good and bad.

The bottom line is that we progress our lines through select individuals, not hordes of birds. We want to breed a higher percentage of good spinners not just MORE birds and get lucky here and there with our mating's. You are on the clock as soon as you stock a bird and if you are not able to utilize them as best you can while they are stocked then you are kind of wasting your time. We just can't assume that our birds will live to be very productive and leave a long lasting impression in our lofts. A lot of this is how you use the opportunities given to you. The time you have to develop a line around key birds is very limited and you can't take any of it for granted.

It is my idea to start small and then build up over time with only good spinners that you can be proud of. This happens very slowly at first and we need to select only the very best birds. We need to gradually increase our breeding numbers from these key individuals and this is where you need to stay focused. Refrain from getting too many birds whenever possible so you can keep things more simple to evaluate the birds you have properly. It's real easy to just breed birds and then toss them to the side for others and start over. However it's an art form to develop birds to your liking and make them extra ordinary. If you do it long enough you can really do some positive things but these things take time and if you are not patient enough it will never happen for you.

You only need a few key birds that are able to produce high percentages of good spinners to make a reliable line of birds. You can start with as few as 3-4 birds and breed for a very long time with just these few and have a lot of success. Many assume you need a whole flock of good birds to win such events like the World Cup but this is not true in the slightest. One thing is set in stone you have to learn how to fly and handle the birds you have and learn to get the most out of them in terms of performance. You need to become a good flyer to be successful in this sport of flying rollers. It will not happen for everyone as many just do not pay close enough attention to what is going on.

I hope that you all are able to get a little insight from this article and I welcome your input, until next time... davesrollerpigeons@gmail.com

In The Spotlight
Interviews in the hobby

***I want to thank George Ruiz for getting me a fantastic interview from Don Macauley and for Don doing a great job with it this interview. It's nice when guys put a real effort in on these interviews as the reader can get a lot more out of it.

Meet Don Macauley- Las Vegas

State your name, age, along with where you live if possible.

I am Don Macauley, 55 years young! I am born and raised in Las Vegas. Been here all my life- so far.

How many breeding pairs do you have and how long do your birds fly before they can become stocked as breeders?

I have way too many breeding pairs. I'll leave it at that!   I fly my birds at least 2 full years before stocking, but it is increasingly difficult to do that anymore with the falcons and also weather changes here in the Las Vegas Valley with very severe updrafts to deal with. I don't stock a bird until into the 2nd year or after a mature moult to see how it does as it goes through maturity and that moult. I love flying quality birds and too often keep flying the best ones on into a 3rd year or more, if I don't lose them before that. I have to be more disciplined about stocking the top quality birds when I should.

Don in Red Rock Canyon with his lucky horse shoe

When did you get started in flying rollers and who helped you initially with your first rollers?

Long story as I knew nothing about rollers when I started. In 1994 I was raising exotic finches. One day I told my wife I was going to get some pigeons as I had some when I was a kid. So I picked up the Nifty Nickel want ads and there it was – roller pigeons for sale. So I went and got a few pair. The guy kept calling me trying to sell me all his birds. Then one day he called and said I could have the birds, as well as all his cages. This guy had show rollers and flying rollers, which I didn't know or care at the time. One of the last birds I got from him had a Hugo Blaas personal band on it. So I called Hugo about the bird and he told me I better call Doug Ouellette in Reno because the bird belongs to him. I called Doug and he was pissed as the guy here in Vegas had this bird on loan from Doug to breed a kit, then was to return them. Instead the guy sold them all in the news paper. Of the dozen birds I had 2 were from Doug, 1 was the Blaas cock, and the rest were show rollers. Over time I became friends with Doug and Don Ouellette. Doug told me about the NBRC and a show called the Pensom Show at the Pomona Feed Store. Back then the CPRC was in what I called their heyday and I went to the show. That was where I met Randy Gibson, Jerry Higgins, and others. Randy invited me to his house to see some birds fly and a barbeque and I ended up staying an extra day. We have been good friends ever since. So I guess the guy that sold the birds out from under Doug I owe my start in rollers, but I will give credit to Doug for getting me my true start in our great hobby. He set me up with his best stuff. I guess it was fate that I just happened to pick up the want ads that day and then happened to get the Hugo Blaas bird with his phone number to get me started! I wear that band around my neck to this day.

What family/strain of rollers did or do you have?

Well, I have quite a few that I am working with, but my goal the next couple years is to narrow it down. My Ouellette birds remain my favorite, but I didn't stock as many as I should along the way so now I am rebuilding those. The best quality I have seen are out of these birds. The few true rare champions I have bred have been out of the Ouellette's, and the Decker's. I also have Tim Decker birds that I am very high on. Again, I haven't built my program with them like I should have, but Tim has been very generous to me with his best stuff. Great quality in his birds. I have some Manny Moreno birds that I am very high on as well. Great quality and Manny is a great guy. He gave me a kit of squeakers in 2012 and the falcon was tearing me up so I ended up stocking what was left. I've been working with them a few years now and very happy with the results. I also have some Willie Wright birds that are good quality and work well together in the conditions I fly in. I acquired some from Willie and when Marlon Garnett got out of rollers I acquired some from him. Willie has built himself a nice family of birds. My latest addition is a stud of Masons. I bought the ones Ellis McDonald donated to the Carolina convention auction, and also met him there. He graciously sent me some more so I would have a stud of the family to work with. This is a new project with the first kit going in the air summer of 2016. I am interested to see if the teamwork they are known for holds true when flown here in the desert and under my management. I also have some South Africans I am playing with, and the odd birds such as a few Horner's, Juan Navarro stuff, Old Plona, Steve Smith/Sal Ortiz, etc. Over the next few years I will be stocking more out of the air. I need to become a better breeder and build my stock loft into proven producers. I have plenty of proven producers, just haven't gone any direction with them. Randy Gibson is a master breeder and flyer, and he has taught me a lot about breeding and building a program, but I haven't listened like I should have! But he has me on the right path after many years of trying to get me going that direction! I can no longer use the excuse that I was new to the hobby and didn't know any better. I almost wasted a whole stud of Doug and Don Ouellette birds by being new to the hobby initially, but also by using that excuse way to long. If it wasn't for my son Richard making me stock birds I would have wasted a whole stud of birds, I would just keep saying **"I will stock it after the next fly…"**

What other strains/families have you worked with and which strain/family worked best for you?

The better question might be what families of birds I haven't I played with! My friend TJ says I need to go to Pigeons Anonymous as seems every time I go to a lawn show or online I am buying auction birds! In a sense he is right as this really isn't the best way to go. I use the excuse that I buy the birds to support the other clubs but I am at a point now where I need to stop acquiring more birds. Just about every auction bird I buy I put in the air, with the exception of a few guy's birds that I am comfortable with putting straight in to stock. Right now the Willie Wright and Marlon stuff is working well for me. With Willie being in the High Desert and Marlon was flying here in Vegas I think we fly in similar conditions and the birds adapt well to my conditions here and handling. I get more teamwork from these birds. The Ouellette's are the best spinners I have seen, when we talk about champion spin. You need to be a master at flying to get the best out of them. I always say I have yet to do the Ouellette birds justice as I have had some great teams of them. My goal is to do that family of birds' justice in the near future, now that I think I have the skills to get that potential out of them. 5 years ago I wouldn't be able to say that. Tim Decker, Manny Moreno, Willie Wright, Steve Smith all have good quality in their birds as well. The few Randy Gibson birds I haven't wasted away also are up there as well. As you can see, with so many birds to work out it is hard to do them all justice as well as stay focused in one direction. I have became pretty good at flying kits, whether mixed families or not, and am ready to take that to the next level of hopefully winning the World Cup and NBRC Fly. I have the knowledge to become a good breeder as well, I just need to focus and do it! I am ready to get that laser focus going. Just about every World Champ and National Champ who has visited me as a Finals Judge or just to visit have one thing in common. They have a small program in which they have created a family of birds that do well in the conditions they fly in and with how they manage them. Heine Bijker put it best to me- He told me I cannot manage the 8 kits I had when he was here. I started to tell him how I fly these kits this day and these kits that day and he said, **"I didn't say you couldn't fly them, I said you can't manage all of them correctly".** And when you reach a certain level of knowledge and ability in this hobby, you know he is right- no matter how much personal pride or resentment you may initially have when someone tells you something like this, in the end he is right.

Champion Spinner from Don's Decker line

What exactly do you look for when selecting breeders? A particular trait or traits?

The first thing I look for is quality of spin in the air, as well as ability to spin with that quality and still kit. I like birds that are not too small or too large.   I have found I don't have to select for that when picking out of the air. The very best ones typically are the medium size ones overall.   A large bird that can be too strong I will probably lose on a overfly updraft somewhere along the way, and a bird that is too small but has the quality of spin I look for typically will not hold up or tire out, and seems like the falcon nails those birds mostly as they get worn out.   I have developed a pretty good eye to select on the ground as well.   I look for a balanced bird that feels good in the hand, has good expression, and just has that look to it, it's hard to describe. You either develop an eye for that look over time or you don't.   There are varying types of outstanding spinners, so if you can develop an eye for the total package vs. one specific type then you have accomplished something special!   William Pensom states in his writings that it takes about 30 years to start mastering rollers. As I start my 21st year I believe him more and more!

What characteristics or traits do you avoid when selecting breeders and flyers?

As I noted above, I don't like too large or too small birds. I don't like birds that won't kit, and I don't like birds that give you problems settling or as their flying progresses. Wire sitters, slow trappers, fast fliers that turn the kit, any bird that gives you a problem from the start usually will give you the same problem as time goes on. The worst are the cocks that are just so cocky they land early or when they land all they think about is strutting around and chasing hens- anything but trapping in and cooperating.   Those overly cocky birds don't last long around here. There are exceptions to this, but I have little patience for problem birds or birds that just don't want to cooperate when the rest are. As youngsters starting out I use patience, but once the kit becomes a kit that flys together and works together, the patience ends and any problem bird has to go after that. Out of those that do cooperate I am looking first and foremost for high quality spin that kit great, as I am looking for birds to make my A team better. Once they make it to my A team and can survive until I am able fly it out properly then I am looking for birds to make my stock loft better.

The best spinner Don has ever seen, Ouellette line shown here at 19 years old

Is there a particular wing style you prefer and why or why not?

I look for a bird that you cannot see the wing position when it spins! If a bird is a blur and balls up, you won't see the wing position. Now of course those birds are rare indeed! So the next tier of spinners would be the H and A style birds, then the V style birds. If the velocity is good, any of the V, H, or A style birds can look good in the air, and it often depends on the angle you are looking at the bird on how the wing style looks. Even an X style bird can look good from the side if the velocity is there, but I am hoping for at least H style or better, with a V style bird with good velocity acceptable if I don't have anything better to replace it with!

Do you recall the best roller you have seen and the best kit you have seen (not including your own birds)? Can you describe this bird and can you describe the kit for us? What made them special or memorable?

The best individual spinner I have seen was at my house. A bird I bred out of a Doug Ouellette pair. She was a recessive red that never went more than 10'. She was a stand still spinner that instantly balled up into a blur when she went into the spin and she just stood in one place nearly while spinning. Took me awhile to spot this bird and she just blew me away. I have seen some great spin at Tim Decker's house. I can think of several I have seen there that I consider champions in the air. Willie Wright and Eric Schoelkopf I have seen some very outstanding spinners that were also deep- 40' plus while holding the spin. But besides the stand still hen I raised, the other bird that stands out in my mind is a bird that my friend Randy Gibson took us to see a fancier named Eugene. I don't know his last name. He had some outstanding spinners and a blue check was hitting it about 15'- just a blur. He asked us each to pick a bird out. My 2 friends went first and they picked much deeper birds. One had their eye on the blue check but opted for a deeper bird. Once he picked I immediately picked the blue check. Randy Gibson said- you got the right one! Eugene was a humble and nice guy. He wouldn't take anything for the birds and let us take the best of what we saw.

The best kits I ever saw was first at Robert Parker's house the year he won the World Cup. His team was like a group of yoyos on the same length string that would set up and go together regularly. The best **team** of rollers I have ever seen was at the 2012 Minnesota convention when Wayne Feder flew his kit. His birds flew a perfect side to side figure 8, with birds breaking on each end of the figure 8. Once they broke all they had to do was fly back up to the middle of the figure 8 to regroup, then would break on the other end of the figure 8. They never had to chase the kit or wait for the kit to come back around after they broke, they just flew back up to the middle of the perfect figure 8 pattern to regroup. We were up on the hill and his kits flew into a nice breeze facing them over the field and they stood in our face for 40 minutes and broke every time on each side of the figure 8. I had never seen birds fly this pattern the entire fly like Wayne's kit did. I don't think the birds were as fast as they initially looked, but they were so smooth and clean in and out of the roll and had enough velocity for me to call them spinners, not just rollers. And the spin is all an illusion so Wayne's kit was very impressive indeed. One other kit performance that stands out to me was at Tim Decker's. It was some event, there were a good number of folks there. But it was windy and his birds got blown off anyway. Everyone had pretty much left to go on to the next house, but since I was riding in the late great Doug Brown's van (the Norco Boys Pigeon Limo- I call it!) I stayed and waited for Tim to be ready to go with us. As his birds made it back over the house all of the sudden they started breaking back to back to back for about a 8 minute period in which they would break, set right back up, and break again. They were going about 15' – 20' at the most with good spin and it was quite impressive. Up until that time I didn't see how a kit could score over about 600 pts based on my interpretation of the use of multipliers, etc. But that show that Tim's kit put on changed my mind on that! When you see kit performance like Robert's, Wayne's, and Tim's that truly stand out you remember them for the rest of your life.

Tell us a little about your preparation weeks and days leading up to a comp fly. What do you feed? How often do you fly?

I am very fortunate to have a great job that usually leaves my mornings free to fly birds. So unless I'm on vacation or at a pigeon fly or event, I am flying kits every morning. Right now my staple feed for all ages of kits is a 14% mix from IFA that has popcorn and safflower. While I continue to experiment with feed, for some reason this mix and this brand works the best for me. Other brands of 14% mix available here just don't work as well for my fliers. I am trying to figure out exactly why! I know that with our dry climate I would get tattered flights and tails on my older proven kit birds. Since using the oily safflower this has all but gone away, except for the few birds that just don't have good feather quality and those I move away from breeding. The key to feeding is to keep control of your birds. Monty Neibel emphasized to me that overfeeding is one of the biggest mistakes made in this hobby. For my young birds I keep them well fed on the mix until they mature, but make sure if they don't trap fairly quickly or fly too long to make adjustments to their rations.

When preparing for a competition fly I start about a month out and pick my 2 best teams of 22-23 birds per kit together. You have to have backups to your first team due to the predator and updrafts here, as well as management mistakes that may cause you to lose birds. I have found it is better not to add to your team as you prepare them for a fly. So the 2-3 extra birds allows me to take some away rather then add. I will move birds from one team to another up to about 2 weeks before the fly, if I have to. The goal is to have the best team in place and not have to make any changes to mess up the kit chemistry. I chart every fly of both kits every day. I note the weather, how birds did, any individual bird notes of problem birds or outstanding birds, and what I fed and how much. I use this chart as a tool to track my management skills and feeding program. It is only a tool though. I have found you have to develop the ability to observe your kit in the air and on the ground to get a true read on their performance and condition. You also have to handle them to check their condition. While it is a team, each bird is still an individual with its own needs. The birds will tell you what they need. The big challenge is learning how to listen to each of them. I use a yoyo system modeled after Monty Neibels' (but in no way as perfected as he had it!) I use the 14% mix as their basic feed, and use wheat and milo to make adjustments. Wheat makes my birds fly higher and longer and I only use it when I let the birds get too under condition too close to the fly. Milo quickly brings out more frequency in my birds and keeps them down. But it also causes the quality to quickly suffer so I have to be very careful with milo. Right now it is my key way to help get my birds ready for a fly. A majority of the top fliers I have visited or talked to use wheat and milo mainly, and rarely the mix. Some use peas as a protein boost. This is the biggest challenge in competing at a high level- figuring out a feed program that brings out the best in your birds. I have gotten decent at this, with the past 5 years having a respectable fly in the big flys more often than not. But still only one time did I feel I got the best out of my kit. That was World Cup a few years ago when I placed in the top 15 and 2nd best in the U.S. My kit was decimated by the falcon and the hodgepodge team I had left was worn out before the finals. I was able to get them in condition and they worked the entire 20 minutes that day. I feel I got the most out of that team that I could. A good feeling, but I am still searching for the magic formula. The more I try to find that fine line of feeding, the more I respect guys like Don Ouellette, Heine Bijker, and Monty Neible who seem to have their teams in top form on the big fly day.

Birds of prey are problematic for most flyers here in the US, how is the bird of prey situation in Las Vegas? Is it a big problem and how many birds would you say you lose every year on average?

Each year here the falcon gets progressively worse. The hawks are in my neighborhood, but are not a threat like in other areas of town and across the country. But the falcon has become a near year round resident and I have only about 3 good months of fly time anymore. 2015 was a very bad year for me with loses. I had several what I call falcon induced overflies and the updrafts this year were very bad. I lost half my yearling team one day leading up to the World Cup, then half my holdover hens a week later. These were 2 – 5 year old birds that had survived just about everything Mother Nature could throw at them, but with the falcon staying under them the higher they go and with the severe updrafts they were lost. Then to top it off I lost half my holdover cock team in early summer. Nothing to do with the falcon, just a summer morning fly in which I let them out and up and away they went. Another group of 2 – 5 yr old birds who had been through it all it seemed. But you never know! Very frustrating but once you release your birds they are no longer yours until Mother Nature returns them to you. So I lock down my best birds as long as I have to. It doesn't do any good to lock down and not fly at all. It only takes a few flys after lockdown before the falcon is back on you. So in order to get my fly fix I release my scrub team first to test the air, and then I usually have another kit of birds like that I can fly, and then a kit of late hatches that I hope can survive the winter. These days late June through early September are really the only times the air is consistently clear enough to fly safely. These months are when I need to really work my young teams and get them well trained before the predators return hot and heavy. So as I think about retirement I dream of somewhere that the air is clear all the time but close enough to wherever my son and family lives to have the best of both worlds for me.

Don's wife shown here with their family dog

Don's son Richard - Dances with Wolves at a local zoo

What various positions have you held, if any, in local, state, or national clubs?

I have been World Cup and NBRC Regional Director a number of times, NBRC President along with the Director at Large role that comes after that. I am starting my 5th year as NBRC Fly Director. And I just took the spot of World Cup North America Coordinator as that remained vacant this year. Since I know most the RD's anyway and have the travel situation pretty much down with my experience as NBRC Fly Director, I think the World Cup job will be fairly easy for me. Still work, but fairly easy- I hope! On the local scene I am the Las Vegas Spinners Club Coordinator. We are starting our 4th year. I was active with the old Las Vegas Roller Club from the time it started, but that club was dissolved as we just didn't get along well overall as a club. George Ruiz and I created the Tribute to Pensom Show here in Vegas, and this will be my 8th year putting that on. We hosted the 50th anniversary NBRC Convention here in Las Vegas in 2011. And somehow along the way I inherited the job of running the annual NBRC internet auction since 2011.

In terms of judging, where have you judged (regions/states) and what do you look for in rollers?

I have judged the San Diego region for the World Cup, part of Texas, and Montana/Canada as well as Northern California for the NBRC Fly. I have panel judged our own region several times. When judging my goal is to be as consistent as possible so that the best kits win and/or qualify. I am looking to score the breaks that are truly scorable- meaning the birds that break together as required and roll a 10 ft minimum roll as required. Then I apply the quality and depth multipliers as accurately as I can.

In the cage I have judged the San Gabriel Valley Spinners Lawn Show, the Northwest Roller Forum show, and the roller class at the Calvacade for Pigeons Show in Fresno. When judging birds in the cage I am looking for the total package bird I described earlier in this interview. I am looking for that bird that has expression and stands out over the others, and more importantly for me it must feel good in the hand. I can pick an outstanding bird out better in the hand then by eye sight. This can be very challenging in a strong class of birds, but you just have to try to be consistent with your standards and pick the bird you feel best meets that standard. I have attended probably about 100 lawn shows and it always amazes me how consistent the different Judges are overall in picking the birds that stand out best. There is no written show standard for rollers. These judges are judging based on their experience and eye for the best spinners they have seen. Amazingly most are quite close on how they pick the best birds in each class.

Beyond just scoring the birds on the flys and placing them in the show cage, I try to make sure and have fun with all the folks, gain and share knowledge, and just enjoy the fellowship of the event. That is the true big prize beyond any trophy or award- sharing the fun of our hobby and the friendships we gain by doing so.

Who has been the most influential person to you in regards to rollers? In other words, who do you consider to be your mentor/s?

Doug Ouellette is my first mentor. He was very straight forward and tough on me when I would call him about the birds, but if you want to fly rollers and compete at a high level then there should be no beating around the bush when it comes to a mentor giving advice. Don Ouellette is the same as his brother. I don't talk to these 2 on a real regular basis but I hope they know how much I have benefited from their advice and blunt approach. Randy Gibson has taught me so much, not only by telling me but showing me as we visited each other and went on flys and to events, Randy is a true master. Tim Decker also has been another I have learned so much from and benefited from his advice. John Vanden Brock as well. The late Doug Brown taught myself and my son so much about genetics during our visits with the Norco group. My son Richard by making me stock the few birds I have along the way, as well as keeping me grounded with common sense and support. A great son and my best friend. Willie Wright I have learned a lot from as well. There are many others but I would say these are the ones that have opened up their knowledge and friendships to me from the first time we met. I am blessed to have them in my life.

What's left over from Don's World Cup team, thanks to the local Falcons and updrafts there in Vegas

Lastly, do you have any additional words of advice for your fellow fanciers?

The first word is PATIENCE. There are no shortcuts to success in flying true Birmingham Rollers. Take your time as you go along. You will find, if you stick to it, that the best birds for you are the ones that adapt to the conditions you fly in and your method of management. As you gain knowledge the birds will benefit from that knowledge. Don't do like I have done and start gathering too many families of birds to the point where you cannot work effectively out of all of them.

Hopefully you can find a mentor who is close enough to you to be able to share their knowledge and support. Don't expect this type of relationship to come easy. First, you must show these masters of our hobby that you are dedicated to your rollers, as well as earn their trust and respect to reach a level of a mentorship relationship. Don't be just a taker. You have to give to receive, and when you give back to the hobby unconditionally you will find you will receive ten-fold back without even asking.

If you choose to put yourself in any leadership role in our hobby, you must be thick-skinned and serve that role in the best interests of the hobby and not let your personal agenda come first while in that role. Don't ever put your birds over any of the great friendships you will gain in this hobby, or in life.

A true champion rollers is rare and hard to replace, but a true champion friend is way more valuable and more difficult to replace. You must possess your rollers, not be possessed by them. If your birds start coming before your life duties to your family, friends, work, or other priorities- then the birds are possessing you. You aren't possessing them. This can be a difficult balance to keep, but you must keep that balance in order to have true enjoyment of your life and your rollers.

Lastly, have fun along the way! This is a very hard hobby to master and will take you a lifetime to potentially become a true master among the other true masters. Whether competing, breeding, backyard flying, or dealing with any negativity-you must have fun along the way. The positives of this hobby far outweigh the negatives. Always remember that. This hobby is really about- the great friendships you make and the fun you have along the way. As I often say **"Enjoy your next fly!"**

Thank you for the privilege of sharing my experiences in this great hobby.

Don Macauley - <u>macsrollers@yahoo.com</u>

Don shown here in the back row with the other flyers in the Las Vegas area

East Texas Spinners

President – Marvin Parks
(409) 779-2666

Vice President – open

Secretary/Treasurer – John Kelly
(903) 245-2030
j.kelly1000@sbcglobal.net

The East Texas Spinners started with 9 members in January of 2012, we currently have 24 members and growing. The club is dedicated to the promotion of the Birmingham Roller throughout region 6A of the NBRC and the Texas region of the World Cup. In addition to sponsoring the NBRC National Championship Fly each fall and World Cup Fly each spring East Texas Spinners hold 2 club flys each year. We also have a picnic and lawn show each October that features a bird auction, raffle, and door prizes. Here is a list of our current members:

Richard Ball - Ferrell Bussing – Carl Braker – Bob & Claudia Choate – Huey Conn – Randy Dotson – Ray Fleming – Errol Forney – Homer Griggs – Alex Hamilton – David Hartman – John Kelly – Charles Kendrix – Joe Mauldin – Doug McCollough – Marvin Parks – Fred Rausheck – Wes Robinson – Walter Stewart – Lloyd Stoy – Don Sutton – Freddie Thomas – Anthony Woerner

South African Imports

By

Dave Henderson

Let me give a brief overview of my personal case before I get to the heart of this article.

Shortly after I got my birds back in 2013 I went on some of the roller blog sites out there and started socializing like many others do daily. I started to reacquaint myself with what was going on in our "roller world" as I had taken a break for the sport of approximately 6 years. I lot had changed since I was last active and this included that both Norm Reed and Jerry Higgins would get out of rollers being the most prominent change to me. There seemed to be a huge demand to obtain specific birds from these lines and guys were willing to pay some big bucks for them, even unproven squeakers.

One of the most interesting things that I discovered looking at World Cup Fly result archives and going back the last 11 years or so, was the flyers in South Africa are a very strong field. Prior to 2007 I really can't even say I recognized South Africa in the field of competitors even though they obviously had been doing well all along. As you dig into more recent archives you will soon see that Croatia and Serbia are coming on as some of the strongest competition in the field also. Until 2015, I had not flown in the World Cup since 2004 and noticed many new countries out there that are putting up some impressive stats and all producing better averages then most here in the US even though we have the highest number of competitors entering every year.

If we look at the number of flyers that are in the Top 5 going back to 2005 here is the way it looks in terms of averages; US 1 per year (38 finalists in 2015), UK .64 per year (6 finalists in 2015), Ireland .82 per year (2 finalists in 2015) and SA 1.27 per year (14 finalists in 2015). This is going back 11 seasons, and South Africa is averaging more than 1 flyer per year into the Top 5. The US has the largest field with 28 regions, UK has 5 regions, Ireland has 2 regions and South Africa has 4 regions. If we push the stats back to the Top 10 or even Top 20 we will see an even stronger dominance by South Africa, but we would see the same with the US and UK.

Getting back to these South Africa imports it just naturally looks like it would be worth the efforts to import birds from there, but just like everything it's not how many birds you get but some key individuals you get that count in the end. So importing a box full of birds from a country is still a large risk when you weigh the cost to do this, and like anything else you have high expectations of these birds when they arrive.

On some of the roller blogs I began to see some talking about these South African birds that were imported to the US, but not many knew much about them. The fancier that had imported them had turned in some impressive flies in 2011 and 2012 in both the NBRC and World Cup. Many that had seen his birds were very impressed by them, but in 2013 this fancier passed away with very short notice due to cancer. I asked a few, "How long did he have these birds before passing away?" I was told he only had them for a few years. I was like "wow… he got results this quick from imports?"

Many times when you import birds, especially from the UK I have seen, the birds have to become acclimated to the conditions here in the US and they consequently won't do so well early on, but over time will get used to the climate and do better, but many don't have the patients. These same fanciers have to learn how to handle these birds as well and this can also play into this. So I think that South Africa must have a similar climate to the Western United States for Ron to have gotten such good results so quickly.

Hannes was also very generous with Ron and sending 14 birds would be a stretch for many fanciers out there and for free no less. Over time Ron and Hannes talked a lot about these birds before he passed and had high expectations with several of them. There are others that have these original imports now and they are still working to figure them out, I think mostly with management and even how to pair them up similarly to how Hannes did it.

I began doing an investigation to learn more about these birds and I was lucky enough to find some who would talk to me about them and I would eventually get to the heart of this birds through Hannes himself. It was not long before I found a handful of fancier that even owned some of these birds here in the US. I learned as much about them as I could. I am now experimenting with a few of my own.

Ron Swart it turns out was a South African citizen that was living here in the US and had married an American women. He had rollers for many years back in South Africa and first got started with rollers in the late 1960's and was born in Johannesburg. He died when he was just 60 years old having lived in South Africa for 50 of those years. Ron came on to the roller scene here in the US nearly as fast as he exited. I wonder how he would be doing with these birds now had he not passed away just 3 years after getting them. This is a question that many I am sure are asking.

The South African Imports were all bred by Hannes Rossouw of Vanderbijlpark Gauteng, South Africa. After communicating with Hannes I soon found out that he shipped the birds in May or June of 2010 and he shipped a total of 14 birds. During transport one of the birds died so 13 made it and 7 of these were old birds and 6 were young birds. While the birds were in transit there was a bird flu outbreak in South Africa which slowed the delivery of the birds a bit, but Ron was still able to get his first young from them out of the nest in December of 2010.

Due to the increased fees of shipping these birds Ron needed help with the importing fees and partnered up with several others to share the birds with. The fees were approximately $770 per bird and after these birds arrived the United States the government banned all live bird shipments coming from South Africa indefinitely, so it is entirely possible that these might be the only rollers that will ever come out of South Africa. In 2015 they tried to ship more birds to the US and they were blocked by the government again.

Ron had a unique way about himself and gave each bird a specific nickname that many will not understand unless they were close friends to Ron. Some that need no explanation would be the *5 second hen* for example. It seems that one pair specifically had an impact of the imports with #220 and #215. There were known simply as "**The Badge Pair**". This pair has shown some great birds with good depth. Others of noted popularity is the Stripe Wing cock and hen.

Both Kelly Applegate and Jim Sherwood told me that some of the very best deep spinning birds they have ever witnessed were some pure South African's close to "The Badge Pair", they were in the 60+ foot range. These tended to develop a little later on average but were very sound birds. Later is really not bad either as they are talking like 7-9 months.

My friend Tim Paustian told me he got some of the first bird from Ron in 2010 and they talked a bit about them. Like anything, you have a learning curve with them and you need to figure out what is working for you with the specific birds you have. You can't expect them all to be good breeders or rollers just because you paid good money to import them. You have to work the birds and select the birds that are working for you. Tim is at the point now where all the birds he is working with are birds he bred and flew out. He is a great guy and has been very helpful with my questions about these birds, even giving me copies of all the pedigrees behind all the imports. He said overall he is pleased with them but has seem some issues with some he doesn't like much, namely the poor breeding instincts of some of the cock birds. He suspects there could be a little inbred depression in some of the birds.

Ron shown here during the 2011 World Cup Finals with Judge Eric Laidler of Denmark

Hannes Rossouw was recently named one of 8 "**Legends of South Africa**". He has taken a couple of years off of competing for personal reasons but assured me recently he will be back in 2017 in full swing. He is still competing at the local level I think just not in the World Cup. **For those interested in learning more about Hannes please check out the 2014 World Cup Yearbook or Spinner Magazine Worldwide Vol 2 which is also available online.**

I came to find out that Hannes' family of rollers were developed from some birds down from Ken White and OD Harris in 1994. (both are now deceased and Legends in the Roller World) Many were breeding pure lines of these families but unsure how many were crossing them like Hannes did back in 1994. Since then there are many experimenting with various crosses there in South Africa to include Mason's like Ron was working with when he passed? These birds were both imported to South Africa sometime in the early 1970's.

Here is the #215 hen from Hannes, she has since died

Here is the badge cock #167

Here is the Stripe Wing cock #168

Jim Sherwood told me last year that he had mostly crosses at one point with the Mollies but had moved to about 90% Pure South African birds only keep 2 mason cocks to mix in as he saw fit.

These imports are primarily dark checker or red checkers but you do get some badges and baldheads at times. They have some very unique characteristics about the eye that I have not seen with any other families of rollers except some almonds I seen years ago from Paul Bradford and you will also see some odd colorations in the feathers like mosaics as well. There is no spread or recessive red in this family from Hannes. It is difficult to say just how these birds might evolve here in the US at this point, but the outlook is very good.

Take a look at Ted Mann from Prosser, Washington. He got his birds from Ron prior to him passing and he is the reigning 2015 World Cup Champion. John Wanless reported Ted's "B" team would have placed in the Top 10 as well, after questioning him about Ted's birds. Ted has found a good program there in Washington and will continue to do well in the future. He says they are strong and he has to fly them hard and the performance never quits with them. If they fly for 1 ½ hours they maintain a constant performance the entire time. He says it took a lot of culling to get him where he has them today and these birds tend to come in early. They have longevity and usually break in big clusters when they go with good depth. He is now breeding all his birds from 9 pigeons that he has discovered are doing the best for him.

I know the birds Ted and others that have these South African's are not native to the US but this kind of gives guys a little more hope that we can accomplish more with the birds that we have here in the United States. I have since heard of many other importations to the US have taken place over the past 2 years and coming have come from several sources. I think guys are yet again trying to get ahead and hope that they can strike some magic with some of these imports.

I was originally interested in these South African's as a possible outcross option for me due to my own family of rollers being ½ OD Harris from some 1980 imports to the US from OD Harris. In the 1st cross I did I think it went very well considering it was just 1 attempt. This season I have several more crosses going to further test this in my loft. The crosses I did last year exceptional birds. They were above all 100% stable, never got crazy or out of control. They started like mine do and slowly got better over time. The awareness in the kit on these crosses was also very good, they were always aware at all time and always performed with the kit.

I had 2 pairs that I bred back to my birds with 2 crosses which would make them ¾ Henderson and ¼ SA. I want to see if they can produce going back. Next season these same cocks I plan to breed back to Pure SA hens making the opposite ¾ SA and ¼ Henderson. As I said it is way too early to be celebrating but due to the fact that I was only able to get back part of my family in their prime I am going to have to create another side of my family so that I can do what I did in the past with the pretzel system.

Although it sounds like Ron might have struck on to something big here with these imports there is still a lot of work ahead for most working with these birds and evaluating them in the stock loft. I think as I said above there is a lot of promise and seeing what Ted has going with his. It's not just exciting for Ted but everyone who is currently working with some of these birds. Time will tell us more.

This little hen is a ¾ Henderson ¼ South African bred from the red check on the next page she is coming in as planned and similar to her father so things right now appear to working as planned in creating a subline

One of the SA crosses I created in 2015 that was outstanding

I would like that thank the fanciers that helped me gather the information for this article to include; Hannes Rossouw, Tou Yang, Jim Sherwood, Ted Mann, Kelly Applegate, Scott Reese, Jay Yandle, Cliff Ball and Tim Paustian.

In The Spotlight
Interviews in the hobby

Meet Aaron Johnson- Canada

Name, age, where do you live; describe your location in Canada and the various climates there where you live

Aaron Johnson I am 42 and live in Kamloops B.C. Canada. This area is a high desert looking area and there are many mountain in my area.

Here is Aaron's home town of Kamloops, B.C.

How long have you been working with your current family of rollers and what various families of birds or bloodlines are behind them?

The strain or family of Rollers I breed and fly today are crossed Pensom's essentially with Stan Plona, Bruce Cooper, Monty Neibel and John Wiens. I have had them for 17 years now, still love what they show me in the air!

A 16 year old cock off Monty's stock

You mention you have birds from Monty and John Weins? How are these birds the same or different? How long since you brought in a new birds from your sources.

This Strain is rich in good blood from careful handling over the years. There is over 40 years behind these birds or more. They are mostly small to medium sized birds. They look like a swallow or resemble one. They are small hard athletic feeling birds. They have what I call a "hatchet keel", they very muscular in the breast, wing tips end a half inch or so from tip of the tail when in the standing position. I would consider these a very well built and balanced Roller Pigeon.

Aaron's hold over kit

What can you tell us about how the birds you have that were bred by Monty? What kind of matings did he like to use. How many birds are behind these birds going back and how long ago was this family created? Please give details on background.

Monty Neibels birds are strong athletic type of pigeon. Looking at these Pigeons you can tell what he was breeding for and that would be high quality high velocity spinners. He always kept things simple and mated one good spinner too another. I was lucky to get a pair from him since there was always a line up of guys wanting birds from him over the years. Monty always bred in an open loft setting, I don't ever recall him using any other methods of breeding. He always claimed he was a better flyer than a breeder. He used a rating system for type and rated the birds from 1 to 5, with 1 being the best.

The lofts of Monty Neibel and John Wiens have contributed great deal of good blood behind my loft today. 95 1592 a Blue Checker Cock and 98 231 a Red Check self hen really helped in contributing to my loft also. The lineage behind these birds is unreal. The depth Monty Neibel and John Wiens had in there lofts would be a dream for many fanciers.

When did you first meet Monty Neible? Tell us about your experience with him from your own perspective of things.

January of 1998 was the year I first met Monty. We were at the residence of Byron Gable who then lived in the Seattle area. You know I really didn't know what to make of him, I think as time went on I got more comfortable being with him on the flies. I had many discussion with Monty on the phone up until he died. He was a character I will say that. He always made trips fun. He held about the rollers and how to manage them. He was true asset to the sport.

Can you share any unique stories that are roller related that many may not have known about Monty? Please fully explain when possible

The one story I recall with Monty was when he stopped by my place on his way too Brian Krogs residence. I Flew my birds for him and we watched them and when they did not trap immediately on landing I was feeling embarrassed and Monty glared at me and said **"Those birds are way too overfed, haven't you been paying attention to them fly them again in 10mins..."** I did fly them again and they did indeed show they were feeling too fine and flew another 45 mins or so. When they came down too land this time they did trap with no hesitations. So from that point on it was a lot of studying and observing the Rollers.

What was the first good spinning/breaking kit you can remember, and who owned this kit?

This question is a no brainer and its Monty's kit in 2000. The kit I called the All-Stars all in full display. I feel so fortunate to have seen this kit and it consisted of 15 hens and 5 cocks. They flew beautifully using the entire sky, stayed right in the yard. You just always knew this guy was as serious as they come with rollers, and always striving to be the best. That's how I'll always remember him the kit broke so big and clean. You could easily make out which birds went and the ones that did not! He scored many halfs and three quarter turns during the fly. The birds were spinning the length of a telephone pole.

Here's Aaron's main loft

What do you think of the general overall quality of the BR today (2015) and how was it different when you first started with rollers? Did you ever get any insight on the rollers in the early days in your region?

I have not been seeing the quality out there, there has been a lot of light tumbling, twizzling, and birds finishing in the wrong direction, but it is not the birds fault, but the Fanciers fault. I have also notice birds missing each other in the breaks, a result from selecting the wrong birds in first place.

I think guys should get back to basic fundamentals and put these methods to use. I think some are just not putting in the time to advance like they should.

What has been the best recent kit you have seen, and how does it compare to what you had seen earlier in your BR career? (If you have a list please list the top 5 or so and what years you saw these kits going back to say 1990)

I would say in no specific order, Rich Hayes-Montana, Rick Schoening-Montana, John Wiens-Canada, Garry Stevens-Washington and Randy Gibson-California just to name a few. All these gentleman fly some very good birds.

Do you fly with a roller club in Canada? What club and how many flyers?

I belong to the Western Canadian Roller Club. Currently there are 12 members with some new Fanciers joining now.

If you could just name 1 person of interest that has influenced you the most over the years with the BR, who would this person be and why?

I would say John Wiens because he's fair, up front and honest with you!

If you could sit down and talk with up to 3, living or deceased, roller flyers and pick their brains, who would they be and what would you want to ask them?

In no particular order, Ollie Harris, Bill Pensom, Bill Richards and Stan Plona. I would be interested in knowing what their favorite birds were, the breeding. Time and management put into their birds. The things they looked for in a high velocity spinner. I would also know what it would take a novice to advance in the sport as quickly as possible.

How many stock birds do you breed from on average each season? How many babies do you produce on average? Do you use foster parents, full time or part time?

Normally I use 6 to 8 pairs of Rollers. I normally breed between 50 and 60 young each season.

Having seen what you have over the years, what do you think the birds are capable of as a TEAM of rollers in a competition? (estimate how the kits will evolve in the next 15-20 years) Do you think that the kits will continue to improve or is it just simply the fact that some can survive more good spinners then others do? Meaning that building up a "hord" of good spinners is mostly due to being able to survive more?

I often find it's the fanciers not the birds that are a problem. Guys need too smarten up and be willing to help each other, and not become enemies. We have to take a bigger look at what we are doing with these Rollers.

Oh I think looking back at Monty Neibel and Heine Bijkers success, sure it can get better. We need to look at the success going on and study what they are doing to get there. I think it's all in the breeding and I think some guys have better luck than others.

What was the best bird you have ever seen flown? Describe it

The best bird, boy that's tough one I have seen many fine birds, the one that comes to mind is a Mealy Self cock, I flew in 2001 he was a wiz in the air! He was very fast and clean.

What have been your best stock birds in your own family? (Attach pic if possible) Describe their characteristics

In my mind they all high quality stock for me and produce great pigeons. I don't recall any one of them standing out from the rest.

Aaron's Bully System cock

What would you say are the most important qualities in selecting a good solid stock bird? (Please rank these qualities by their importance to you)

I look for that bird that is fast and very swift, it looks graceful, a real standout in its performance. It must be always consistent and kit fantastic.

What advice would you give to any would be roller flyer that is open minded out there wanting to fly in better rollers?

Novices need to be very careful when looking for birds as this inexperience can cost them, not just money but time as well. Its' wise to check the fly lists published on the World Cup fly archives or in the NBRC to locate some known flyers. Many just starting out are really not aware of these organizations until later on, so this is part of the issue. Once you find some guys go see their birds fly and see multiple flyers and ask them questions about others in the area too, where they would go to obtain birds if they were looking? Try to learn the lineage behind these birds and how to manage them properly.   You need to be able to switch the pairs around so are you able to find the birds that produce the best for you and start to learn how to pair the birds up. Ask for advice and really listen to what is told to you. When looking at fast rollers here are things to look for;

1 Short Keel
2 Sharply Pitched Keel
3 muscle mass tone
4 Short arm bones
5 narrow flights
6 short primaries
7short secondaries
8 tight feather
9 sparse feather
10 narrow tail
11 short tail

What has been the most memorable trip judging rollers? How did they compare to what you know in your own region?

Most memorable judging trip I did was going too Ontario, Canada. I must say and I have to be honest here, I was not impressed at the overall quality of the birds I seen there in Ontario. I 0bserve all kinds of faults in the majority of the kits flown, at best I saw average mediocre Rollers and nothing that really caught my eye. What I did notice is that these fanciers were made too believe they were flying good birds and they were not. I noticed a lot of mistakes happening there and it would have been a good experience for a novice flyer in what to look for in culls to see in this breed. There was twizzling, tumbling, birds dropping out, birds rolling down in the yard, or rolling out the wrong direction after the break the list goes on.

Some of these guys have been in the hobby for a long time and some just don't get along at all. This is not good for a region and the birds usually suffer because of this. I expected more from these guys. They should know better than this. I did see some fanciers that had potential to do well but they are going to have to be careful what they breed from in their lofts.

Pigeon politics and making enemies in the same region is not good for anyone and we need to figure out a way to get this sort of thing behind us when it happens.

Visit this site to read the book about James Turner of South Carolina

Nice water color rendition of Michael Spiegelberg's bird he named Poison. Bred by David Curneal

The Birmingham Roller Pigeon
Information for the book

I was looking over a lot of old roller bulletins and magazines in recent months and discovered this very cool information that will give you the ability to label your copy of "The Birmingham Roller Pigeon" so that you will be able to identify the photos displayed in the book. This is invaluable information and is a real bonus.

This information was first submitted by Gene Giegoldt who is at present the Band Secretary for the National Birmingham Roller Club (NBRC).

Gene states that this is the absolute latest information in regards to the photos displayed in Pensom's book and this information was gathered in part by Tom Monson, Dick Stephens and Howard McCully. There are still some photos that not identified and it is entirely possible that we will never know what birds this are and by whom they were bred.

If there are some out there that have any data on the birds that are in the book that have not yet been identified please come forward and give us the information so that we can complete this list. I will leave contact information of Gene at the end of this article to give you the ability to contact him should have information in this regard.

Here is the information that will list the page the photos is in the book and listing the information about the bird on these pages;

This version is an edited version to maximize space I plan to resubmit the long version to the NBRC very soon as I have retyped this entire document.

BOOK INFORMATION LISTED BELOW:

COVER: MRS 1925 #521 – This is Bill Pensom's old Crystal Palace Champion.

Page 3, Top: PRC 1957 #231 – Blue check mix wing hen owned by Lester Lehmeyer

Page 3, Bottom: unknown # - Red check badge cock bred by Pensom.

Page 4, Top: unknown # - Red-necked hen bred by Pensom and was a deep spinner.

Page 4, Bottom: PRC 1958 #5167 – Champion dark blue check mix wing cock bred by Pensom and sire of the white ticked hen NBRC 1959 #4512 when it was mated to the "Red Headed Hen".

Page 7, Top: NBRC 1934 #743 – Dark check self hen, bred by Pensom. Imported to the United States along with HRC 1933 #699 white self cock. This pair was owned by JL Smith

Page 7, Bottom: NBRC 1936 #13 – Cream bar badge hen bred by Pensom. Winner of 12 shows, also a quality spinner.

Page 8, PRC 1951 #664 (double banded) JLS 1951 #60 – Red check badge w/ender cock bred by JL Smith. "Champion and sire to Champions"

Page 13, PRC 1955 #183 – Mealy dun bar self cock bred by Pensom.

Page 14, Top: PRC 1955 #106 – black bronze cock.

Page 14, Bottom: PRC 1956 #109 – Champion red check badge hen, bred by Pensom.

Page 19, Top: Red Spangled hen **no band listed**

Page 19, Bottom: Blue bar bald butted w/ender hen and **no band listed**

Page 20, Top: PRC 1956 #1226 - Silver red bar badge cock bred by Doug Stephens from Pensom stock

Page 20, Bottom: PRC 1958 #3844/JLS 1954 #91 – "Champion" Red check white wing bred by JL Smith. Double banded with an old JLS band.

Page 25, Top: 1958 #5287 – Dark check white wing hen, bred by Ralph Hilton of North Hollywood, California.

Page 25, Bottom: unknown # - Dark check white flight, mixed tail hen bred by Pensom. "Champion Spinner for 10 yards"

Page 26, Top: Tortoiseshell cock, **band is unknown.** This bird was bred out of #876 and #4121 Tortoiseshell grizzle family, Brother to PRC 1956 #955

Page 26, Bottom: PRC 1952 #2709/JLS 1952 #9 – "Old JLS Champion". Dark check self with bronze cock, double banded.

Page 31, Top: unknown # - Recessive red whiteside beard hen bred by Pensom. This bird is thought to have been PRC 1957 #6350

Page 31, Bottom: PRC 1952 #4356 – Dark check self cock bred by Dr. Charles Rivers.

Page 32: Unknown # - Red badge w/ender, son of Ken Payne's Champion Red badge cock shown on page 56

Page 37, Top: NBRC 1955 #1305 – Ken Payne's "champion", blue check badge hen.

Page 37, Bottom: Unknown # - Blue check badge w/ender hen, Bred by Pensom

Page 38, Top: Unknown # - Bleu grizzle hen bred by Pensom and a "Champion Spinner for 10 yards"

Page 38, Bottom: PRC 1956 #1824 – Tortoiseshell hen bred by Doug Stephens.

Page 43, Top: PRC 1955 #7061 - Blue grizzle cock bred by Stan Plona.

Page 43, Bottom: Unknown # - Dark Tortoiseshell white wing hen.

Page 44, Top: RLP 1948 #38/PRC 1948 #1448 double banded – lavender mealy badge cock with heavy black flecking, bred by Ray Perkins.

Page 44, Bottom: PRC 1951 #1830 – "Champion" blue bar white wing hen bred by Pensom.

Page 49: PRC 1955 #5135 – Black grizzle neck white wing hen, "Champion Spinner for 10 yards".

Page 50, Top: "The Whitney Cock" PRC 1954 #3543 – Dark check self cock bred by George Whitney from Pensom stock.

Page 50, Bottom: "Red Headed Hen" PRC 1958 #255 – Black pepper-head hen bred by Pensom

Page 55, Top: PRC 1958 #201 – White self cock stolen from Pensom's loft in 1959. This cock was later returned and was supposed to go to Dick Stephens after the 1966 season.

Page 55, Bottom: PRC 1952 #4235 – Champion black mix wing cock bred by Lester Lehmeyer and looked very similar to PRC 1956 #145

Page 56, Top: NBRC 1955 #1304 – Ken Payne's champion red check badge w/ender cock. Sire of red badge cock shown on page 32

Page 56, Bottom: Unknown # - Red bar grizzle hen. This bird was said to be bred by Pensom and to have an example of "Poor Expression" and a "Cull"

Page 61, Top: PRC 1959 #2745 – Dun (mealy) badge hen and Champion bred by Henry Lopez of Bell, California.

Page 61, Bottom: Unknown # - White self out of #876/#4121

Page 62: PRC 1952 #1912 – Grizzle hen. There is some questions about who bred this bird and it is said to have been either Stan Plona or John Spuria.

Page 67, PRC 1956 #182 – Black mottle white wing hen bred by Pensom

Page 68: Yellow badge w/ender white eyed hen bred by Pensom. Suspected as being PRC 1957 #233. **Page 68, Bottom:** Blue check w/ender ticked hen, not bred by Pensom. Pensom said this hen had "Ideal Expression"

Page 73, Top: Unknown # - Black mottle cock, not bred by Pensom

Page 73, Bottom: Unknown # - Red check badge mix wing hen

Page 74: NBRC 1943 #369 – Blue check badge hen a Champion Imported by Chandler Grover thru Pensom.

Page 79, Top: PRC 1957 #4990 – Red check badge cock bred by Pensom. This champion cock was known as "The Old One-Eyed Cock"

Page 79, Bottom: PRC 1954 #3569 – Black self cock bred in George Whitney's loft.

Page 80, Top: PRC 1950 #2713 – Blue check badge champion cock bred from PRC 1947 #1232 ($350 cock) and JLS 1942 #25 a blue check white wing hen.

Page 80, Bottom: Unknown # - Red mottle white side

Page 85: PRC 1953 #514 "The Pensom Famous 514 Hen" – Dark check bronze self and champion performer and outstanding producer.

Page 86, Top: Unknown # - Black self cock not bred by Pensom

Page 86, Bottom: Unknown # - Red check bald w/ender hen

Page 91: Stan Plona, J Leroy Smith, Bill Pensom at Conoga Park, CA

Page 92, Top: Unknown # - Black mottle hen not bred by Pensom

Page 92, Bottom: PRC 1959 #5610 – Red white wing cock bred by Pensom

Page 103, Top: Unknown # - Silver Red Bar self hen. Pensom said "Hen is ideal type and expression"

Page 103, Bottom: Unknown # - Dark check bald butted wing hen bred by Pensom

Page 104, Top: Ruben George's Loft in Chicago Height, Illinois

Page 104, Bottom: Howard McCully's Loft in Portland, Oregon

Page 109: Unknown # - Yellow badge butted white-eyed hen bred by Pensom (could be PRC 1957 #236)

Page 110, Top: Unknown # - Red check white wing hen bred by Pensom

Page 110, Bottom: PRC 1954 #2420 – Red grizzle cock bred by Al Calloway Las Vegas, NV

Page 115, Top: Unknown # - Pensom's Champion red marked hen

Page 115, Bottom: PRC 1951 #578 – Champion dark check self cock bred by Stan Plona

Page 116, Top: PRC 1956 #2266 – white self hen bred by Pensom

Page 116, Bottom: NBRC 1936 #7 – Champion Recessive red badge hen bred by Pensom

Page 121, Top: NPA 1949 #16970 – Dun Mealy beard cock bred by Wayne Maust of Long Beach, CA

Page 121, Bottom: PRC 1947 #274 – Black badge white wing hen bred by Ciro Valenti of Kansas City

Page 122: PRC 1954 #1769 – Champion blue bar badge white wing cock bred by Stan Plona

Page 127: PRC 1957 #206 – "The Unrung Hen" A champion blue check badge hen

Page 128, Top: PRC 1958 #17 – Light tortoiseshell grizzle hen bred by Dick Stephen

Page 128, Bottom: Unknown # - Blue grizzle white wing hen bred by Pensom

As noted above this is just a simplified version of Gene Giegoldt's article and there are still 25 birds shown on this list that are unknown of their exact band number. If anyone else is out there that may have this information please contact me or Gene with the appropriate information to research at. However based on the time that this information has been unavailable it may never be known.

National Birmingham Roller Club
Founded 1961

2016-17 Officers

President
Nick Siders
Contact:
nsiders203@sbcglobal.net
870-739-2269

Vice President
Jon Farr
Contact:
wishiwon2@yahoo.com
208-374-5202

Director At Large
Cliff Ball
Contact:
cballdds@yahoo.com
366-601-6877

Secretary-Treasurer
Jay Alnimer
Contact:
jaystarroller@yahoo.com
440-258-2909

Publishing Editor
Bob Simpson
Contact:
NBRCPubEd@aol.com
828-713-5148

Band Secretary
Gene Giegoldt
Contact:
cpbw56@hotmail.com
805-522-7363

Accessory Secretary
Kenny Libick
Contact:
libicks@aol.com
682-224-4647

Publicity Director
David Curneal
Contact:
djcurneal@aol.com
435-754-7841

Website Director - Norm Brozovich - broz50@comcast.net

Printed in Great Britain
by Amazon